"Ray Comfort has delved into the heart of the personal lives of The Beatles, an area which many authors deliberately avoid–into the controversial subject of their personal faith. He has taken a thorough, historical approach to his research into the cultural and spiritual impact of the greatest band the world has known."

DAVID BEDFORD, AUTHOR OF *LIDDYPOOL: BIRTHPLACE OF THE BEATLES*

"A celebrity's spiritual life has always been a topic of interest in the eyes of fans and media. I can definitely relate because of my three year ministry work in Hollywood evangelizing famous celebrities. Now with The Beatles, we get a fascinating look at the nature of fame and the universal longing of the human heart, which is the search for God. In *The Beatles, God, and the Bible,* you will understand the significance behind this search, and why it pertains to you specifically. This entertaining, informative, and enlightening book should be widely read, discussed, and reflected upon, whether you are a Beatles fan or not. It could indeed change the direction of your life."

STEVE CHA, AUTHOR OF *HOLLYWOOD MISSION: POSSIBLE*

"A generation later, we are still feeling the effects of The Beatles' spirituality. In his clear, incisive style, Ray Comfort helps us understand why the band that had everything on earth wanted something more. Even better, he helps us understand why it matters to us now."

PASTOR BRUCE GARNER, HUNTINGTON BEACH, CALIFORNIA

"It grieved me to learn that Paul and John completely turned their backs on the church of their youth. And then John wrote one of the worst songs ever penned, 'Imagine,' which was very anti-Christian. Now, my friend, Ray Comfort, examines the side-effects of this cultural phenomenon, which resonate even today."

KEN HAM, PRESIDENT, CREATION MUSEUM AND ANSWERS IN GENESIS

"Always compelling, Ray Comfort uses little known facts and stories about John Lennon and The Beatles to drive home truths you will never forget. I have known Ray for many years and in all those years I have never ceased to be amazed by his ability to take the common lessons in life and turn them into the most common sense understanding of the gospel message I have ever heard. *The Beatles, God, and the Bible* will surely not disappoint."

STUART G. SCOTT, SONG OF THE YEAR, GRAND PRIZE, KSBJ, 1985

"I have had the highly unique privilege of working under Ray Comfort's mentorship and what can I say? If God had a SEAL Team six of his own, Ray would be on it! Ray's love and dedication to researching the topic of *The Beatles, God and the Bible* is second to none. Whether your knowledge of The Beatles is nominal or phenomenal this book is sure to unveil a side of them you never knew!"

CHAD WILLIAMS, FORMER U.S. NAVY SEAL, AUTHOR OF *SEAL OF GOD*

THE BEATLES
GOD
& THE BIBLE

THE BEATLES
GOD
& THE BIBLE

RAY
COMFORT

WND Books

THE BEATLES, GOD, AND THE BIBLE

WND Books
Washington, D.C.

Book Designed by Mark Karis

Photographs by Alexander Turnbull Library, Wellington, New
Zealand and Mitchell Library, State Library of NSW (Call no.
Australian Photographic Agency - 16583 and 16690)

WND Books are distributed to the trade by:
Midpoint Trade Books
27 West 20th Street, Suite 1102
New York, NY 10011

WND Books are available at special discounts for bulk
purchases. WND Books, Inc., also publishes books in electronic
formats. For more information call (541) 474-1776
or visit www.wndbooks.com.

First Edition

Print ISBN: 9781936488551
eBook ISBN: 9781936488919

Library of Congress information available.

Printed in the United States of America.

To my wonderful sister—Chris Diedrichs—
who was there when I needed her.

"I'm not afraid of death because I don't believe in it. It's just getting out of one car, and into another"

*~ **John Lennon***

• Table of Contents •

• Acknowledgments •

My sincere thanks to Manuel Brambila for his valuable research; to editor Lynn Copeland; and to WND, for having the vision to publish this series.

KEN MANSFIELD

*I*N THE DIFFICULT TASK of tackling the oft-deliberated subject of John Lennon and God, Ray Comfort deals more in the illusions of the subject than its conclusions. It is hard to pin down Lennon the man, Lennon the rock star, Lennon the philosopher, Lennon the seeker, Lennon the skeptic, and Lennon the grown-up with a boyhood that clings intensely to his mental framework. That is the short list of the perspectives one must consider when taking a long look at someone who becomes almost bizarre, when all the words are added up. Ray comes at the subject matter from the outside, ends up inside, and then turns it all about, and spreads the results at your feet. He does what he does best and uses God Almighty as the anchor in exploring the stormy life of someone larger than life . . . but not bigger than Jesus. There are many sharp angles to the Lennon story . . . this one rounds off some of the edges so you can grab onto the intent of the author's message. No matter what you think about the person under the microscope in this treatise, it would be hard to imagine there was no Lennon.

~ Ken Mansfield, Author/Speaker, Former U.S. Manager of Apple Records

*T*HERE ARE SOME WHO BELIEVE that one of the Beatles signed a pact with the Devil, and that was why they achieved instant, worldwide fame. I tend to believe it was because their music was good. *Really* good.

I can remember the very moment I heard them sing, back in 1963. Their music gave me spontaneous joy. Amazingly, after all these years, it still does. From the opening twang of "A Hard Day's Night" to the bouncy sound of "Penny Lane," each song recalls immediate and pleasant memories. They are like markers of time—bringing with them large deposits of nostalgia that, for some reason, don't have the usual twinge of sadness.

I also remember how good I felt when I walked with friends to the movies in our black, high-heeled, pointed-toed Beatle boots. We felt like kings.

Today, I often find myself on the Internet, watching fans scream as Paul and George shake their hairy heads as they sing, Ringo pounding the drums, and listening to John's amazing voice. He was so gifted. Although I don't think I ever purchased even one of their records, I am a self-confessed closet fan of the early Beatles.

I hope you enjoy reading this book as much as I enjoyed writing it.

~ *Ray Comfort*

THE BEATLES:
A MINI HISTORY

*I*N THE SUMMER OF 1956, a fifteen-
year-old from Liverpool, England, and some
friends formed a skiffle group[1] called the
Quarrymen. The ensemble soon began experiencing
moderate success playing at parties and in contests,

and their popularity quickly grew.

On July 6, 1957, shortly after a major performance at an outdoor party, the band played during a garden fête[2] in the field behind the St. Peter's Church, Woolton, Liverpool. The band members were John Lennon (guitar, vocals), Eric Griffiths (guitar), Colin Hanton (drums), Rod Davis (banjo), Pete Shotton (washboard), and Len Garry (tea chest bass[3]). The event featured music, crafts, cakes, a police dog demonstration, a float parade, and the traditional crowning of the Rose Queen.

The fête, the yearly highlight in Woolton Village, started at 2 p.m. with several flatbed lorries (freight trucks) driving slowly around Woolton and back toward the church. The first lorry, all in pink and with long ribbons, carried the Rose Queen on her throne, along with several other girls, all chosen from Sunday school groups because of their good behavior and age.

The next lorry carried the Quarrymen. The band, standing on the back of the cart, tried to play as they passed down the streets, but were having difficulty staying together. Finally, John decided to sit and hang his legs over the edge as he played and sang. He soon gave up, though, as no one could hear him.

At 4:15, the Quarrymen moved from the lorry to a permanent stage, where John performed a song titled

"Come Go with Me," which he'd heard on the radio. He didn't know some of the lines in the verses, so he made them up. John stood out from the other members.

The Quarrymen were scheduled to play again that evening, at 8 p.m., at the "Grand Dance" in the church hall. They would alternate onstage with the George Edward Band. The ticket price was two shillings.

Several hours before the dance, Ivan Vaughan, John's neighbor, childhood friend, and sometime–tea chest bass player with the Quarrymen, introduced Paul McCartney, his fifteen-year-old classmate from the Liverpool Institute, to the group. Paul was wearing a white jacket and black pants.

Paul and John Lennon became instant friends, and that afternoon, Paul showed John how to tune a guitar. (Up to that time, John and Eric had tuned their guitars to John's mother's banjo.) The two chatted briefly, and then Paul performed a couple of songs for them, including "Twenty Flight Rock" by Eddie Cochran, and a medley of songs by Little Richard. John was impressed with Paul's natural talent. The teen could easily play songs that had been hard for the Quarrymen to perform.

Of that day, bass player Len Garry said, "We've all got different versions of this. I remember Paul doing a Little Richard impersonation, and I said to

John, 'That's good—let's get him in.'"[4]

About two weeks later, Paul was asked to join the group as a guitar player. He later said, "I knew the words to 25 rock songs, so I got in the group. 'Long Tall Sally' and 'Tutti-Frutti,' that got me in. That was my audition."[5] Paul then asked John to invite his school friend George Harrison, who was just fourteen, to join them as the lead guitar player in February 1958.

On one occasion, the group was invited to play thirty-minute sets between bingo sessions at the Pavillion Theatre in Lodge Lane. In the interval, Lennon, McCartney, and Hanton had too much beer and when they were riding a bus back home, Paul criticized Hanton saying that he wasn't a good drummer. Hanton physically attacked Paul. After the fight was stopped, Hanton was helped off the bus, together with his drums, and was never contacted again.

In January 1960, Stuart Sutcliffe, a friend of John's, joined the group, playing bass guitar. Around this time, the band began exploring alternative names for the group. Sutcliffe suggested "the Beatals," as a tribute to Buddy Holly's group, the Crickets. After experimenting with several other names, the band settled on "The Beatles" in August.

But the four Beatles were missing a drummer,

having lost Hanton the year before, so they auditioned and hired Pete Best, who was very popular with girls.

In 1960, the band's unofficial manager, Allan Williams, took the group to Hamburg, Germany, when another group he managed proved successful there. The Beatles initially lived in an unheated storeroom, in a bad area of town, renowned for gangsters and prostitutes.

The group played regularly at a series of four different clubs in Hamburg between August 1960 and December 1962. During this time, they improved their performance skills and gained a reputation for their unique style of music.

In 1961, Sutcliffe, an art student, decided to continue his studies in art, so he left the band, and Paul had to fill in the position as a bass player.[6]

Back home in Liverpool, the Beatles established themselves as the top local band, earning the attention of Brian Epstein, a music-shop entrepreneur, who later said of the band, "I was immediately struck by their music, their beat, and their sense of humor on stage—and, even afterwards, when I met them, I was struck again by their personal charm. And it was there that, really, it all started."[7]

Epstein began courting the Beatles and, hoping

to secure a recording contract for the group, made a number of trips to London to visit different record companies. He was rejected by many.

On New Year's Eve of 1961, the group was driven to London for an audition with Decca Records, but their driver lost his way, and the trip ended up taking ten hours. The audition finally took place on January 1, 1962, when the band, in just one hour, performed fifteen songs. Decca executives informed the Beatles that they would know the results a few weeks later.

Eventually, Decca did let them know. They said that "guitar groups are on the way out" and "The Beatles have no future in show business."[8]

Epstein, by now the group's manager, then persuaded record producer, arranger, composer, and musician George Martin to listen the band's demo. Epstein was offered a contract, even though the Beatles had previously been rejected by almost every other British record company. Martin later said it was Epstein's enthusiasm and his unwavering confidence that the Beatles would one day become internationally famous that convinced him to sign them.[9]

In June 1962, the band recorded their first single, "Love Me Do," at their first recording session at EMI.

After the session, George Martin informed their manager that he didn't want Pete Best to play the drums the next recording session. He didn't suggest that he be replaced permanently, but the other three Beatles had already been thinking of terminating him. This is because he was shy and didn't like their hairstyles. John Lennon said, "We were cowards," because they left their manager with the job of firing him. They then hired Richard Starkey, better known as Ringo Starr.

Their second single, "Please Please Me," recorded in November, became their first number-one hit, and by 1963, what was termed "Beatlemania" had overtaken Great Britain.

John Lennon and Paul McCartney had established a good songwriting partnership. Though most of their songs were signed "Lennon/McCartney," usually the song's author sang the lead vocal. Brian Epstein's advice on how to behave onstage helped the group, and they spent most of 1963 touring, while their first album, *Please Please Me*, recorded in a single day, remained the top seller for an amazing thirty weeks. It was finally displaced by their second album, *With the Beatles*.

In October of that year, Ed Sullivan, host of the highest-rated variety show in the United States, was in London. At the time, the Beatles were returning to England from their Swedish tour, and the resulting tumult caused delays at London's Heathrow Airport. When Sullivan, also at the airport, discovered the reason for all the commotion, he made a note of the group's name.

Two weeks later, the group's manager went to New York and was able to meet with Ed Sullivan, who booked them for three shows. This was *before* the Beatles even arrived in America. Meanwhile Sullivan received more than fifty thousand requests for its 728 seats in the CBS auditorium—even more than he got for the 1956 appearance of Elvis Presley.

On February 7, 1964, approximately four thousand fans showed up at London airport to see the Beatles leave for the United States. Their 1963 single "I Want to Hold Your Hand" had sold an unprecedented 2.6 million copies in the U.S. during the previous two weeks. Another three thousand people waited for the band at New York's JFK airport. Soon they would appear for the first time on American TV.

On February 9, 1964, as more than 73 million viewers tuned in to *The Ed Sullivan Show*, Sullivan announced in his characteristic stoic fashion, "Ladies and gentlemen, the Beatles!" The next day, the Beatles performed at the Washington Coliseum, then appeared a second time on *The Ed Sullivan Show*. Beatlemania was established in the United States.

By this time, the band held twelve positions on *Billboard* magazine's Hot 100 singles chart, including the top five songs. Their songwriting, particularly that of John and Paul, just kept getting better and better, as the two were known to engage in a bit of friendly rivalry.[10] The Beatles' incredible success in the States created a renewed interest in Britain's music, and soon other British artists began to explore the American market. This period is known as the "British Invasion."

After their successful first tour of America, The Beatles returned to London to be greeted by huge crowds of screaming fans, where they conducted an interview with the British media:

Q: But what did you do? Did you just do all the same routine as you do here?

Paul: Er, yeah.

John: We did the older songs.

George: Most of our records are hits over there.

Paul: Oh yeah, we had to do "Please Please Me" over there. We hadn't been doing that for a long time here, but it's in the charts there.

Q: That's history, here. What about The Beatles' styles, all these wigs and suits and things? Are they catching on over there?

George: Yeah, they're selling well.

Ringo: Fifteen million a day!

Q: I hear that the four of you have been million-aires by the end of the year.

George: Oh, that's nice.

Q: Have you got time to actually spend this money?

The Beatles, in unison: What money?[11]

The group started to tour internationally, and were warmly welcomed everywhere they went. They gave thirty-two concerts in nineteen days in Denmark, the Netherlands, Hong Kong, Australia, and in beautiful New Zealand. They then went back to the United States and gave thirty concerts in twenty-three cities.

But there was a problem: their amplification equipment was not powerful enough to be heard over the screaming fans. At times, the Beatles couldn't hear their own performances, and neither could the audiences. Soon, touring became nothing more than a boring routine for the group.

In March 1964, the Beatles were offered a motion picture deal, and in summer 1964, *A Hard Day's Night*—a mock-documentary in which the band members played themselves—premiered in London and New York. The movie's plot begins with the Beatles running from fans, and going by train to London to appear on television. After a number of interruptions, the group ends up in the baggage cart, trying to find some peace and quiet. When they arrive in London, they are taken to a hotel, where they feel trapped, so they set out for a little adventure, in which Paul's grandfather causes trouble at a casino. After a night on the town, the band is taken to a theater, where they are to be filmed before a live audience. Performance preparations take some time, during which Paul's grandfather encourages Ringo to go off by himself to experience life. This throws the rest of the group into a panic as they try to find their lost drummer. In the meantime, Ringo is arrested by the police, but finally returns, much to the relief of the rest of the Beatles, and the performance goes on as planned.

The film was an international success, as was its accompanying soundtrack album, *A Hard Day's Night*. This record was followed by the album *Beatles for Sale*, recorded in the late summer and fall of the same year.

In April 1965, John and George tried the hallucinogenic drug LSD. Ringo and Paul then followed.

It's important to understand that during the 1960s, LSD was at first considered a harmless drug. But perhaps a little history is in order.

LSD: A SHORT HISTORY

Swiss chemist Albert Hofmann was the first to synthesize LSD, or *lysergic acid diethylamide*, on November 16, 1938, in the Sandoz laboratories. Five years later, its psychedelic properties were discovered when, on April 16, 1943, as Hofmann was studying and resynthesizing the drug, he was forced to interrupt his work and go home. Writing of the experience, he said that he felt:

> affected by remarkable restlessness, combined with a slight dizziness. At home I lay down and sank into a not unpleasant intoxicated-like condition, characterized by an extremely stimulated imagination. In a dreamlike state, with eyes closed (I found the daylight to be unpleasantly glaring), I perceived an uninterrupted stream of fantastic pictures, extraordinary shapes with intense, kaleidoscopic play of colors. After some two hours this condition faded away.[12]

"Possibly a bit of the LSD solution had contacted my fingertips," he wrote later in his autobiography, "... and a trace of the substance was absorbed through my skin."[13]

Hoffman decided to self-experiment three days later to understand LSD's true effects. He intentionally ingested 0.25 micrograms, the smallest amount he expected would produce an effect. Within an hour of taking the drug, Hofmann experienced rapid changes in perception. His laboratory assistant took him home on a bike, since cars were forbidden at that time due to war restrictions. On the way, Hofmann struggled with anxiety, thinking that his neighbor was an evil witch, that he was crazy, and that LSD had poisoned him. When the doctor arrived, the only thing he noticed was Hoffman's dilated pupils. As his terror faded away, a sense of joy kicked in as, he wrote, "little by little I could begin to enjoy the unprecedented colors and plays of shapes that persisted behind my closed eyes. Kaleidoscopic, fantastic images surged in on me, alternating, variegated, opening and then closing themselves in circles and spirals, exploding in colored fountains, rearranging and hybridizing themselves in constant flux."[14]

Sandoz Laboratories brought LSD to the attention of the United States in 1949, as they believed it could have medical uses. The drug was used by psychology students as part of their education during the '50s, and *Time* magazine published six positive reports on the drug from 1954 to 1959.

LSD was restricted by the government, and its use became illegal by the mid-'60s. Considered to be affecting people's values, LSD was declared

"Schedule 1," meaning that the drug had "high poten-
tial for abuse" and was without "currently accepted
medical use in treatment." It was removed from
circulation, and the USDEA (United States Drug
Enforcement Administration) said,

> Although initial observations on the benefits
> of LSD were highly optimistic, empirical data
> developed subsequently proved less promising . . .
> Its use in scientific research has been extensive
> and its use has been widespread. Although the
> study of LSD and other hallucinogens increased
> the awareness of how chemicals could affect the
> mind, its use in psychotherapy largely has been
> debunked. It produces aphrodisiac effects, does
> not increase creativity, has no lasting positive
> effect in treating alcoholics or criminals, does not
> produce a "model psychosis," and does not gen-
> erate immediate personality change. However,
> drug studies have confirmed that the powerful
> hallucinogenic effects of this drug can produce
> profound adverse reactions, such as acute panic
> reactions, psychotic crises, and "flashbacks,"
> especially in users ill-equipped to deal with such
> trauma.[15]

On October 6, 1966, LSD became illegal in California, and other states and countries followed after.[16]

That same year, John Lennon and Paul
McCartney wrote the song "Lucy in the Sky with Dia-

monds" for the Beatles' album *Sgt. Pepper's Lonely Hearts Club Band*, which was released in 1967. By this time, John had a toddler son, Julian. Little Julian was said to be the inspiration for the song, after he brought home a nursery school drawing that he called "Lucy—in the sky with diamonds." However, after the song's release, some began to speculate that the title was a subtle reference to LSD, no doubt because of the Beatles' much-publicized experimentation with the drug (not to mention that the first letter in each of the three nouns in the song title spell *LSD*). Though John denied this and mocked the idea that the title contained a hidden drug reference, the British Broadcasting Corporation (the BBC) banned the song.[17]

Soon the speculation became international. In the midst of this, the Beatles continued to insist that the title was inspired by John's son's drawing, and the Lucy in that drawing was a real person, Julian's classmate Lucy O'Donnell. Years later, Julian himself said of the sketch, "I don't know why I called it that or why it stood out from all my other drawings, but I obviously had an affection for Lucy at that age. I used to show dad everything I'd built or painted at school, and this one sparked off the idea."[18]

In 2007, the real Lucy O'Donnell told the BBC, "I remember Julian and I both doing pictures on a double-sided easel, throwing paint at each other, much to the horror of the classroom attendant . . . Julian had painted a picture and on that particular day his father turned up with the chauffeur to pick him up from school."[19] She added later, "As a teenager, I made the mistake of telling a couple of friends at school that I was the Lucy in the song and they said, 'No, it's not you, my parents said it's about drugs.' And I didn't know what LSD was at the time, so I just kept it quiet, to myself."[20]

In further interviews about the song, John said he was disappointed about the arrangement of the recording. He lamented that he had not taken adequate time to fully develop his idea for it, adding that he also thought he didn't sing it very well. "I was so nervous I couldn't sing," he said, "but I like the lyrics."[21]

In 1971, Lennon stated in a *Rolling Stone* interview that he had no idea the song's initials spelled out the word *LSD*. "I didn't even see it on the label. I didn't look at the initials. I don't look—I mean I never play things backwards. I listened to it as I made it. It's like there will be things on this one, if you fiddle about with it. I don't know what they are. Every time after that though I would look at the titles to see what it said, and usually they never said anything."[22]

And later, during David Sheff's 1980 interview with John Lennon and second wife, Yoko Ono, for *Playboy* magazine, Lennon said again, "My son Julian came in one day with a picture he painted about a school friend of his named Lucy. He had sketched in some stars in the sky and called it 'Lucy in the Sky with Diamonds,' simple."[23]

Cynthia Lennon, John's first wife and the mother of Julian, corroborates his story. In her biography, *John*, she remembers the day Julian came home with the picture. "He had come home from school with a painting of his friend Lucy," she wrote. "When John asked him what was in it, he'd said, 'It's Lucy in the sky with diamonds.' John, of course, loved this way-out and completely innocent description, straight from his son's unfettered imagination."[24]

However, during a newspaper interview in 2004, Paul McCartney was quoted as saying, "'Lucy in the Sky,' that's pretty obvious. There's others that make subtle hints about drugs, but, you know, it's easy to overestimate the influence of drugs on The Beatles' music. Just about everyone was doing drugs in one form or another and we were no different, but the writing was too important for us to mess it up by getting off our heads all the time."[25]

Despite their drug use, in June 1965, the Beatles

received the Members of Order of the British Empire (MBE) award from Queen Elizabeth II.

The next month, the band released their second film, *Help!* This movie was also accompanied by an album, on which the Beatles began to incorporate classical instruments in songs such as "Yesterday." It became the most recorded cover version of any song in history.[26]

In August, the Beatles visited the United States for the third time, performing at the Shea Stadium before a massive crowd of 55,600. This event, at the peak of their career, was the first major stadium concert in history.

At this point, the band began to weigh two options: they either had to continue to produce the same type of music that had made them such a success, or take a risk and explore other styles and areas to evolve as musicians. They choose the latter, and their next album, *Rubber Soul*, is regarded as a leap of maturity in the group. John and Paul's competition over songwriting became more evident and pushed them to their creative limits.

In August 1966, they released *Revolver*, which continued to bring new and different sounds to what had become known as "popular music." By then, the Beatles had played more than 1,400 concerts, over a four-year span, around the world. Even so, a week after *Revolver*'s release, the Beatles concluded their final tour at Candlestick Park, San Francisco. The consensus was that, from that point on, they would only record albums. One reason for this was that the sounds and techniques used in the studio were so sophisticated, they were hard to re-create in stadiums.

In February 1967, the Beatles released their new single, "Strawberry Fields Forever," from *Sgt. Pepper's Lonely Hearts Club Band*, which took more than 700 hours of studio time to record. The band wanted the album to sound different from anything they had recorded in the past, and it certainly did. *Sgt. Pepper's Lonely Hearts Club Band* mixed elements from jazz, rock and roll, music hall, and traditional Indian music. The Beatles hired other talented musicians and used innovative production techniques. They sang about childhood, aging, day-to-day routine, and postwar Britain's life. The album's tone ranged from cheerful to ironic to transcendental to the surreal. And fans around the world, in efforts to find hidden meanings and deep sense, analyzed not only every lyric, but also the album's widely popular cover, which pictures the Beatles as a fictitious band, posing in front of a collage of famous people.

The album was a commercial success, and it

remained at the top of the U.K. Albums Chart for twenty-seven weeks, and fifteen weeks on the *Billboard* 200 in the United States. It won four Grammy awards in 1968, and is considered a defining album for the psychedelic rock style and one of the most influential albums in history.

Even today, *Sgt. Pepper* is considered one of the "greatest albums of all time."[27] In 2003, *Rolling Stone* magazine gave it the number one spot on the list of "500 Greatest Albums of All Time." It is also one of the best-selling albums in the world, with more than 32 million copies sold.[28]

On June 25, 1967, the Beatles performed on the first live worldwide television broadcast, *Our World*, playing their newest single, "All You Need Is Love," which became a hallmark of that time. An estimated 400 million people watched the show in twenty-four different countries.

Around that time, the group shifted to psychedelic influences by using marijuana and LSD, and to further learning about Eastern thought. Later in 1967, they met the Maharishi Mahesh Yogi and went to Bangor to follow a Transcendental Meditation retreat.

While they were in Bangor, they received some shocking news. Brian Epstein was dead! He was only thirty-two.

At the official inquest, his death was ruled an accidental overdose of the barbiturate Carbitral. Epstein suffered from insomnia, and it was discovered that he had swallowed six Carbitral tablets in order to sleep, before being found dead in his locked bedroom on August 27, 1967. Apparently, six tablets was his usual dosage, but his tolerance for the drug meant that it was very close to lethal.[29] Therefore, it was believed, his death was caused by a steady and gradual buildup of the drug in his system, mixed with alcohol. But rumors soon began to surface that he had committed suicide.

Epstein's passing left the group without direction and not knowing what to expect from the future. In his comprehensive and revealing 1970 *Rolling Stone* interview, John revealed that their manager's death was the beginning of the end for the Beatles. He said, "I knew that we were in trouble then."[30]

Their next project was the *Magical Mystery Tour* album and movie. The album, released in December 1967, received good reviews, but the movie, directed mostly by Paul, garnered the group's first major negative press in the UK. Another movie, *Yellow Submarine*, a humorous cartoon featuring the Beatles and their songs, was released in June 1968. The album of the same name came out in 1969.

It was then that the Beatles turned to the Maharishi Mahesh Yogi as their guru, since Epstein was gone. In a later interview, John would say that they looked on the Maharishi as a "father figure."[31]

Some time later, they left the Maharishi. Rumors had begun to spread about him making sexual advances toward female participants in his three-month "Guide Course." The band also felt that the Maharishi was using them for his own publicity, so they parted ways with him. But their time under his spiritual guidance is considered one of their most creative periods, as they recorded thirty songs for their double album known as the "White Album" because of its white cover (the album's official title was, simply, *The Beatles*).

Unfortunately, this period was also characterized by a number of conflicts between group members. Ringo left for a time, leaving Paul to fill in on drums for some songs. John then lost interest in the group and in writing with Paul. He had evolved as a person and as an artist, with new vision and interests, including his romance with Japanese-American artist Yoko Ono. (Soon Yoko convinced John to sponsor some of her exhibitions, and he agreed to help as an anonymous donor.)

Around the same time, Paul met Linda Eastman,

a photographer and big Beatle fan. She became pregnant, and the two were married on March 12, 1969. The marriage was devastating news for female fans around the world.

John began bringing Yoko to the recording studio, disturbing the atmosphere in which the band was accustomed to working. Given their disunity, the *White Album* ended up being filled with mostly individual projects, backed up by the rest of the members. These recording sessions were regarded by the Beatles themselves as the beginning of their breakup.[32]

Yoko encouraged John to move on to new things. By then, John spent most of his time with her, but he was still forced to find time to come to the studio and record with the band. It was apparent he wanted to leave the group. He recorded and released two songs on his own ("Instant Karma!" and "Cold Turkey"), and also formed a group called the Plastic Ono Band, which performed in Toronto's Rock and Roll Revival. He was ready to quit the Beatles, but legal ties kept him in.

From October 1969 until March 1970, Paul took a long break because he wanted to spend time with his family and his new daughter. It was during this time that a DJ in Detroit announced that Paul had died in an accident and that an impostor had replaced him. The "Paul is dead" rumors spread widely, and to this day, fans try to find hidden messages and clues to solve what they believe to be a mystery.

The Beatles' last recorded album was *Abbey Road*. By this time, relations between the Beatles were so sour that John requested that Side A of the LP be recorded with only his songs; side B, with Paul's. Despite his request, the band recorded a complete side with individual Lennon/McCartney songs and Side B with a medley, as George Martin had suggested.

The album received mixed reviews, not only from the press and fans, but from the Beatles themselves. Still, *Abbey Road* sold five million copies in the first year, which was two million more than *Sgt. Pepper*.

The Beatles final performance, the famous *Let It Be* concert, was given on the rooftop of the Apple Corps building in London on January 30, 1969, during lunchtime. The band played for forty-two minutes, until the police shut them down due to noise complaints from people who obviously weren't fans.

On April 10, 1970, Paul McCartney officially announced his departure from the group. Shortly after this, on May 8, the Beatles' final album (though mostly recorded before *Abbey Road*), *Let It Be*, was released. For this project, Paul decided to perform and record live, in front of an audience. The album was released together with a film, which clearly showed how the Beatles had disintegrated. This was the lowest point in the Beatles' relationships. None of the group attended the premiere. It was a sad day for Beatles fans.

But an even sadder day would come for those who loved John Lennon.

JOHN LENNON & GOD

Life is what happens to you while you're busy
making other plans.[1]

*~ **John Lennon***

HEN JOHN WINSTON LENNON,
born on October 9, 1940, was still very
small, and while his father, Alfred, was
away at sea during World War II with the merchant
navy, John's mother, Julia, had an affair with a soldier,

who got her pregnant. She gave birth to a baby girl, who was put up for adoption. She then met another man, and asked Alf for a divorce, but he wouldn't agree to it. So, still married, John's mom went to live with the other man, "in sin" (as it was called in Liverpool), and had two daughters by him. After John's aunt Mimi twice complained to Liverpool Child Services, his mother allowed her sister to take John to live with her and her husband at their home. John grew up resenting his mother.[2]

Aunt Mimi sent John to an Anglican Sunday school at St. Peter's Church in Woolton, where he sang in the choir, but when he turned eleven, he was banned from it because he "repeatedly improvised obscene and impious lyrics to the hymns."[3]

Twenty-six years later, on March 4, 1966, John conducted a casual interview with the *London Evening Standard*, a British newspaper, that was picked up on March 21 by *Newsweek*. Speaking of the Beatles, he said, "We're more popular than Jesus now . . . Christianity will go, it will vanish and shrink. I needn't argue about that. I'm right and will be proved right."[4]

Here is the context of his words from the 2,145-word article: "He still peers down his nose, arrogant as an eagle, although contact lenses have righted the short sight that originally caused the expression. He looks more like Henry VIII than ever now that his face has filled out—he is just as imperious, just as unpredictable, indolent, disorganised, childish, vague, charming and quick-witted."[5]

It then seems, from the article, that this was the beginning of the Beatles' interest in Hinduism. The writer portrays Lennon as excited by its music and possibly the religion itself:

> George has put him on to this Indian music. "You're not listening, are you?" he shouts after 20 minutes of the record. "It's amazing this—so cool[.] Don't the Indians appear cool to you? Are you listening? This music is thousands of years old; it makes me laugh, the British going over there and telling them what to do. Quite amazing." And he switched on the television set.
>
> Experience has sown few seeds of doubt in him: not that his mind is closed, but it's closed round whatever he believes at the time. "Christianity will go," he said. "It will vanish and shrink. I needn't argue about that; I'm right and I will be proved right. We're more popular than Jesus now; I don't know which will go first—rock 'n' roll or Christianity. Jesus was all right but his disciples were thick and ordinary. It's them twisting it that ruins it for me." He is reading extensively about religion. . . .
>
> He paused over objects he still fancies; a huge altar crucifix of a Roman Catholic nature with IHS on it; a pair of crutches, a present from

George; an enormous Bible he bought in Chester;
his gorilla suit.

Later that year, the American teen magazine
Datebook printed the quote once again, but this time
it had far-reaching repercussions. Suddenly, radio
stations in America's "Bible belt" were banning The
Beatles' music, and the national news media were
showing clips of teenagers smashing and burning
Beatles albums. There were even threats on the band
members' lives.[6]

> Most Americans had taken Lennon's remark
> about Jesus as offhandedly as it had been
> intended, but the South had not. There had been
> a wave of anti-Beatles demonstrations, Beatles
> albums were burned in community bonfires, and
> no fewer than 35 radio stations observed a boy-
> cott of Beatles music. The Beatles' 1966 tour of
> the South was their last. They were pelted with
> rubbish and frightened by firecrackers thrown
> at them onstage.[7]

John was understandably bewildered by the
hostility, because what he said was true, from his
perspective. The media of international television and
radio had given the Beatles instant worldwide popularity. From a historical perspective, the crowds that

followed Jesus were limited to the land of Israel and were in the thousands, but the Beatles were loved by *millions* around the world. Remember, in the United States, an estimated 73 million Americans tuned in to watch *The Ed Sullivan Show* in 1964, when the group made their first U.S. television appearance.

But there's another reason Lennon thought that the Beatles were more popular than Jesus, and that Christianity was dying. Sure, from the American public's perspective, Christianity was alive and well, and Jesus wasn't simply a historical figure who said some interesting things. He was the only Lord and Savior, so their knee-jerk reaction was to ask who this arrogant upstart was, who had grown too big for his own Beatles boots. But contemporary British Christianity in John Lennon's day was extremely different from the faith of the average American. British culture is quiet, conservative, and may even seem a little dull to outgoing America. Consequently, both the traditional Protestant and Catholic church services in 1960s England were a little dull, with dull hymns and dull, monotone priests and ministers who preached dull sermons to a group of sad, elderly people. They sat in a cold stone building called a "church" that was appropriately surrounded by a graveyard. And there you have Christianity from the perspective of a young John Lennon. It was dying, if not dead, and Jesus Christ was simply an interesting but historical figure who had little relevance to contemporary British youth, who were going wild over the Beatles. The average British teenager was about as interested in British Christianity as a toddler was in studying Shakespeare written in Pig Latin.

John's words, in America, could be compared to a smiling traveler quipping, "I've got a bomb in my briefcase," as he passed through metal detectors at New York's airport on September 12, 2001. Those words would have had little meaning or repercussion if uttered in the privacy of the traveler's home in another country. But spoken in a New York airport the day after the tragedy of 9/11, they would have been taken very differently. The outspoken Beatle's words were hardly noticed in Great Britain, because Brits understood his perspective. But they were a big bombshell in the United States.

No doubt, John was pressured by his record company to make some sort of apology. The statement meant the loss of millions of dollars in record sales. So, six long months later, on August 11, 1966, a meek (and still mystified) John Lennon held a news conference in Chicago. He said:

If I had said television is more popular than Jesus, I might have got away with it, but I just happened to be talking to a friend and I used the words "Beatles" as a remote thing, not as what I think—as Beatles, as those other Beatles like other people see us. I just said "they" are having more influence on kids and things than anything else, including Jesus. But I said it in that way which is the wrong way."

Reporter: Some teenagers have repeated your statements—"I like The Beatles more than Jesus Christ." What do you think about that?

John: Well, originally I pointed out that fact in reference to England. That we meant more to kids than Jesus did, or religion at that time. I wasn't knocking it or putting it down. I was just saying it as a fact and it's true more for England than here. I'm not saying that we're better or greater, or comparing us with Jesus Christ as a person or God as a thing or whatever it is. I just said what I said and it was wrong. Or it was taken wrong. And now it's all this.

Reporter: But are you prepared to apologise?

John: I wasn't saying whatever they're saying I was saying. I'm sorry I said it really. I never meant it to be a lousy anti-religious thing. I apologise if that will make you happy. I still don't know quite what I've done. I've tried to tell you what I did do but if you want me to apologise, if that will make you happy, then OK, I'm sorry.[8]

Steve Turner, author of *The Gospel According to the Beatles*, said:

> I think John Lennon was surprised because it had been said in a casual way to a journalist who was a personal friend of his and he had no idea it would cause that sort of controversy. When it did happen he was actually quite frightened because they were about to go off on tour and there were these threats to their lives and a clairvoyant made some predictions that their plane would crash. It was really quite frightening and they wanted to cancel the tour but they knew they couldn't. They were under obligation to the tour promoters. And when he made his apology in Chicago, (the band's) press officer told me that John was actually in tears before he went in to make the apology.[9]

When asked if he thought John's apology was a sincere one, Turner replied, "His apology was very carefully worded. He never said, 'I didn't mean that'; he kind of said, 'If it was taken that way, that's not what I meant,' but he never actually retracted it. The reason it happened that way, in America particularly, is that people thought The Beatles were getting too big, too proud, and it was a way of putting them down and I think people grabbed that opportunity."[10]

John's sister, Julia Baird, said, "How can anyone

have misconstrued what he said? I felt desperate, we all did, for John at that time. He never meant it like that. He said, 'Oh Julia I never, never meant to offend anybody at anytime with that remark,' and it was as big a shock to him as anything else."[11]

It was unfortunate that from that point, John Lennon gained a reputation for being anti-Christian. The Beatles were such a phenomenon that fans hungered to know anything and everything about them, and the media obliged. Yet, think about this: Who of us would come out unscathed if every area of our lives were probed? It would only be a matter of time until we said something we regret or something that could be misinterpreted. Contrary to popular belief, John said, "People always got the image I was an anti-Christ or anti-religion. I'm not. I'm a most religious fellow."[12]

Still, it's almost impossible to change public perception, despite John's pleas for people to believe he was anything but anti-God. In an interview with *Playboy*, he was asked, "You're quoting one of your peers, of sorts. Is it distressing to you that [Bob] Dylan is a born-again Christian?" John responded:

> I'm not pushing Buddhism, because I'm no more a Buddhist than I am a Christian, but there's one thing I admire about the religion: There's no proselytizing.[13]

In other words, John didn't appreciate Christians' efforts to recruit unbelievers.

So, exactly what faith *did* John have? We'll explore that question in the next chapter.

· 3 ·

JOHN'S FAITH

I was brought up a Christian and I only now
understand some of the things that Christ was
saying in those parables.[1]

~ *John Lennon*

OST PEOPLE BELIEVE in God's
existence. It's hard not to, with all of
His amazing creation staring us in the
face. Still, there are some who deny their God-given
common sense, close their eyes to creation, and

believe the unscientific thought that nothing created everything. Atheists can't have their cake and eat it, too. Either something made everything, or nothing made it.

Despite the fact that a young Paul McCartney had once quipped that none of the Beatles believed in God, Lennon was a deeper thinker. He later qualified Paul's belief that they were all atheist by saying that the Beatles were "agnostic": "We're not quite sure what we are, but I know that we're more agnostic than atheistic."[2]

Of his personal beliefs, John said, "I believe in God, but not as one thing, not as an old man in the sky. I believe that what people call God is something in all of us. I believe that what Jesus and Mohammed and Buddha and all the rest said was right. It's just that the translations have gone wrong."[3]

His perception of "God" being "something in all of us" is easy to understand. Human beings are not like animals, or birds, insects, and fish. All of these, including us, have senses, circulatory and digestive systems, appetites, a will to live, and a need for rest. But there is something unique about the human race. We are *moral* beings. Fish don't have court systems. Neither do animals, insects, or birds. If one of their kind transgresses some moral law, the rest don't seek retribution. They don't have a judge and jury, and they don't punish a guilty comrade.

But humankind certainly does. Our species will go to the ends of the earth and spend billions of dollars to bring the guilty to justice. This is because we are made in the image of God. We have His likeness engraved upon us in that we know right from wrong. Lennon therefore understandably expressed this uniqueness as being "God" in all of us. He said, "We're all God. I'm not *a* god or *the* God, but we're all God and we're all potentially divine—and potentially evil."[4]

He didn't mean that we were each the Creator, or even a lesser god. He was saying that we have the propensity to do good and evil, and we have a God-given inner knowledge of when moral boundaries are crossed. The Bible explains this as the "work of the law" being written upon our hearts (Romans 2:15). This is a reference to the moral law (the Ten Commandments). This work of the law is the echo of the human conscience. None of us can plead ignorant as to the basic issues of right and wrong. Rather than say that it is "God" within us—that is, His divine presence—the Scriptures tell us that it's His divine stamp.

This is why John rejected atheism.

In 2008, in a lost radio interview from 1969, John encouraged people to focus on the Christian faith:

> Despite his familiar image as a hippy icon who invited us to imagine a world without religion, Lennon says he was "one of Christ's biggest fans" and felt emotional in church. . . .
>
> Christians around the world had been dismayed by Lennon's boast in an article in London's *Evening Standard* about the popularity of the Beatles, but the singer says he was misunderstood.
>
> "It's just an expression meaning the Beatles seem to me to have more influence over youth than Christ," he says. "Now I wasn't saying that was a good idea, 'cos I'm one of Christ's biggest fans. And if I can turn the focus on The Beatles on to Christ's message, then that's what we're here to do."[5]

In the same interview, John said that people overreacted to his comments, adding, "If the Beatles get on the side of Christ, which they always were, and let people know that, then maybe the churches won't be full, but there'll be a lot of Christians dancing in the dance halls. Whatever they celebrate, God and Christ, I don't think it matters as long as they're aware of Him and His message."[6]

Continuing, he acknowledged a strong belief in prayer, and like most people, he didn't like hypocrisy, saying, "Community praying is probably very powerful[.] I'm just against the hypocrisy and the hat-wearing and the socializing and the tea parties."[7]

At the age of fourteen, he was banned from church by the local victor because he and his friends were giggling. "I wasn't convinced of the vicar's sincerity anyway," he said of the incident. "But I knew it was the house of God. So I went along for that and the atmosphere always made me feel emotional and religious or whatever you call it." Unfortunately, in his own words, "Being thrown out of church for laughing was the end of the Church for me."

CREATION, SAM, AND LENNON

Elton's gonna die young. I'm gonna be a ninety-year-old guru.

~ John Lennon

L ET ME TELL YOU about my dog. I do so to make an important point. If you aren't a dog lover, please bear with me.

When our dog died, we decided that we would live dog-less for a time. I'm the dog lover in our family, and it wasn't long before I began using pictures of puppies to talk my wife, Sue, into getting a puppy. Soon we located a litter of the cutest bichon pups.

As we were looking at them, the owners asked if we wanted to meet the father of the litter. We said that we would. A door was opened and a fast-moving father ran around the room like a maniac, then was quickly ushered into another room. We picked a pup, and as we were walking out the door, the owner said, "Good luck." That was a little strange, but it was a statement that would come back to haunt us.

It wasn't long until Sam, the cutest little dog you have ever seen, was part of our family. It was a joy to once again hear the pitter-patter of little paws around the house. Knowing that Sue wasn't the type of person who would ever think of letting a dog lick her face (the sign of a true dog lover), I resolved to show my own appreciation for his place in our home by being quick to clean up after him.

Sam was the most wonderful-natured dog I have ever had. If he was chewing a bone and you got too close, he would stop eating, lick your hand, and then bring his bone closer to you so that you could be a guest at the table.

There was only one problem with him. He was an idiot. As he grew, he would run at you. Not to you.

At you. If you were sitting on a couch, he would run across your shoulders, and even sit himself on your head. More than once, he ran at a portable table on which I had placed a full cup, and put his paws on the table. Each time, I would yell, "No!" at which point he would push away, sending the hot liquid flying.

Every night, for about two hours, he would go literally crazy—running around the house like a mad dog with the energy of a two-year-old on steroids, jumping on and off of Sue's lap, around her shoulders, down the hall, and back again. It was no exaggeration to say he was "bouncing off the walls." He used the couches to defy gravity as he bounced off of them. He chewed our furniture, chewed windowsills, got pictures off the walls and chewed them, and ripped up any paper he could find. He would go through the trash bin, open cupboard doors, and lift container lids to eat chocolate brownies (five at a time). He wet the bed (not his—ours), burst out the front door onto the road if given half a chance, cry if he was left downstairs at night, whimper outside our bedroom door upstairs at night, drive visitors crazy, scratch with his claws, lick with his tongue, whine with his whiner, and he would even get on top of the kitchen table after a meal and sneakily eat any leftovers. I guess he learned this after he learned how to climb up onto the kitchen counter and eat any food he could find. Worst of all, he would take food off my plate while it was still on my lap! If I disciplined him, that was obviously a game, which sent him into more tail-wagging excitement.

A game he loved was staring you down, but if he thought you were winning, he changed the game to "lunge at the nose." When he went to the groomers', they would graciously say he was "a handful." The vet called him "feisty." Once, he chewed the corner of my wallet; he regularly emptied it with vet fees. Often, we would lie awake at night and hear him get into the cupboard where we kept our pots and pans. I guess the cupboards reminded him of the chocolate cake he once ate in similar cupboards, upon which we had to put kiddie locks.

If I sat down to answer the phone, he would get jealous and whine. If I tried to walk around during the conversation, he would wrap himself around my legs as I walked. He did the same thing anytime I tried to walk downstairs. And he would throw himself against our bedroom door in the early hours of the morning and scare the living "nightlights" out of us.

I would continually tell Sue that it was just a matter of time until he matured. We could work it out. Meanwhile, I diligently taught him to sit, lie down, jump, roll over, and shake hands. The only command he didn't obey was "Stay." And that was the one that mattered. It drove us to off-the-charts stress levels. An elephant doing cartwheels each evening in the living room would have been less disruptive.

In an effort to keep the peace between Sue and Sam, I would make excuses for him—he's tired; he's young; he's still learning. But one evening, I was left excuseless. That was the time Sue was feeling really exhausted after a hard day's night. She dropped herself down on her favorite place to sit—our soft leather couch. Unfortunately, Sam had deposited Lake Superior on her seat. She sat in it and was coldly soaked to the skin. He had the whole house to use as a bathroom, and he choose that spot! I couldn't justify it. I should have known better.

Sam had to go.

I needed a little help from my friends. I offered Sam as a gift to one friend who loved him. He would sit on a chair and let Sam run all over him and even sit on his head. My friend, actor Kirk Cameron, who starred on the TV sitcom *Growing Pains* and movies like *Fireproof* and *Monumental*, said he would talk it over with his wife. A couple of days later, he graciously said she wanted a larger dog. I then offered Sam—plus five hundred dollars cash for dog food—to my buddy Mark. Mark politely turned me down. I next offered him to another friend Brad, with a thousand dollars for dog food. He said he would give it some thought and talk it over with his wife. Soon, though, he respectfully rejected my offer. It looked as though Sam was staying.

By his first birthday, believe it or not, there had been some real improvement. However, one day I was working in my garage/workshop when I heard a sound with which dog owners everywhere are familiar. This was about a month after he pulled the lid off some glue and ate half of the contents. Fortunately, it congealed and came back up as a rubber ball about the size of a small child's fist. This day, Sam was again making the now familiar "I'm getting ready to give dinner back to you" sound. I yelled, "No! Sam, *don't.* Go outside, now! Onto the lawn. *Now!* Go!" He didn't even look at me. He completely understood that I didn't want him throwing up in the garage, and quickly headed toward the door. He was being obedient, even in the middle of his suffering. How I love obedience. What a good dog. He ran through the garage door, turned sharp left when he hit the lawn, charged up the steps, through the little doggy door, into the house—and threw up on our living room carpet!

CREATION, SAM, AND LENNON

But the worst came about a week after his first birthday. I had spent hours filming in Santa Monica in Southern California. It was even worth the three hours on the freeway to get there and back. I had one great interview that was good enough to make it onto the TV program I cohost.[1] These are few and far between. Returning home, I left the MiniDV on my desk in my home office, planning to "log" it the next day. It *really* was a great interview.

When I arrived home that day, I found, to my horror, that Sam had chewed the cassette. I decided to try to save the tape, and put it into a new casing. After two to three hours of meticulous work, I finally did it. I slipped it into the camera to see if it would rewind, and it jammed the camera! I now had no tape, and it cost $250 to get it removed from the camera.

All that to make one important point. This life is full of Sams. You know that. Nothing is simple. We move from one Sam to the next. Everything has some sort of bruising kickback. All any of us want is to be happy. Yet ask any human being if it's a struggle to hold on to happiness, and he or she will list enough problems to leave *you* with a problem—depression! There's minor health issues, aging parents and the complications that go with it, sick kids, financial pressures, marriage problems, doctor's bills, someone

49

close has cancer, a widow needs help, rebellious kids, headaches that have no real cause, not enough rain, too much rain, insurance companies that won't pay up, lawsuits, neighbor problems, a rotten boss, mother-in-law problems, addictions, guilt, nightmares, fears, worries, pains, sores, rust, accidents, cockroaches, termites, fleas, pollution, earthquakes, tornadoes, hurricanes, endless tribulations, and more waiting in line to hit you tomorrow. One day you are singing, "All my troubles seemed so far away," and the next, you are looking for a place to "hide away."[2]

So, what's going on? Did God create man to have nothing but problems, that, try as he may, he can't seem to avoid? Then, after the unavoidable pains of old age (even for the rich and famous), it all ends when death comes—that's unless some terrible disease or horrible accident kills him in his youth, before he even reaches sixty-four. The odds of that happening are pretty high. Every month throughout this sorry world, 490,000 people die of heart disease; 218,000 of cancer; and 116,000 of respiratory diseases. And every *year* 1,202,000 die in traffic accidents; 399,000 through falls; 365,000 people are drowned; and over two million die from sexually transmitted diseases.[3]

But there's good news for those who ask what on earth is happening. This world is *not* as God planned it. We live in a "fallen" creation. In the beginning, everything was perfectly good. Adam's "Sam" obeyed. At first, his fruit didn't have worms. His soil didn't have weeds. There were no tornadoes, suffering, dentists, disease, decay, or death. All that stuff—along with morning sickness and labor pains—came as a package deal through the rebellion of Adam and Eve. When sin came—the world's "Sam"—so did the Genesis curse and all the pain and problems we see every day (see Genesis 3).

Without a belief in the Bible's book of Genesis, humanity has no explanation for its origins, nor does it have any explanation for our continual sufferings. Atheists believe that nothing created everything, and then to explain everything, they maintain that evolution, without a mind or even a reason, brought about flowers, birds, trees, seasons, fruits, clouds, the sky, the perfectly positioned sun, magnificent mountains, cold snow, the saltwater seas, freshwater lakes, the cleansing rain, plus the right mixture of oxygen and hydrogen to sustain life. Fortunately, gravity just *happened* to be present to make sure everything didn't spin off into space. Add to that a million and one other coincidences that make life possible, and you have the dream world of the atheistic evolutionist. It's not evolution that is mindless and unreasonable; it's its believers. They don't think too deeply. They don't give thought to the fact that we have insects, fish, birds, animals, and people, *all* with corresponding male and female genders, and all with the ability to bring forth after their own kind.

On top of all of this, the atheistic evolution believer looks down his condescending nose at anyone who believes in God, and thinks that what he believes has something to do with "science." Evolution is the epitome of audacity. The only "science" about it is that it's science fiction.

There is no indisputable proof of any species transitioning into another species. After two hundred years, Darwin's missing link is still missing. Pressure an evolutionist for empirical evidence for the theory and all he will have is disputable unsubstantiated transitional forms and a nebulous list of references to mutations and bacteria.

However, those who have good old common sense know that a creation is empirical evidence of a Creator, and, with a little research, that the Bible is axiomatic. It is the *self-provable* Word of the Creator of all things. It gives explanation concerning our origins. God made the heavens and the earth. We don't need to search the depths of outer space for clues as to where we came from. Just read the Book.

God made male and female, and He caused each of them to bring forth after their own kind (Genesis 1:20–27). And that's what we clearly see in creation and in the fossil record. There are no half-evolved animals. Everything is fully formed and functioning, male and female, bringing forth after their own kind. It's no wonder that the Beatles soon backslid from being atheists.

Psalm 90 begins by explaining God's eternality and His creative power: "Lord, You have been our dwelling place in all generations. Before the mountains were brought forth, or ever You had formed the earth and the world, even from everlasting to everlasting, You are God. You turn man to destruction, and say, 'Return, O children of men.' For a thousand years in Your sight are like yesterday when it is past, and like a watch in the night" (Psalm 90:1–4).

God dwells outside of the realm of time and space. He dwells in eternity. You and I have to wait for time to pass, but the Bible tells us that God created time and that He Himself isn't subject to its restrictions. We are held within its dimension, but God is not. He can whisk through time and tell us what is going to happen in the future.

John Lennon at least once tried to do that himself in a recording session with record producer Phil

Spector:

> **Lennon**: What are they gonna do, play jazz with Jethro Tull?
>
> **Spector**: No, Elton John, probably.
>
> **Lennon**: Elton is good friend of mine.
>
> **Spector**: Well, it's good. He's got the same name as you, only you spell it in front and he spells it in the back. And you both go to the same place.
>
> **Lennon**: No, no, no, no, I refuse. Elton's gonna die young. I'm gonna be a ninety-year-old guru.
>
> **Spector**: Okay. I make history, you make gurus.
>
> **Lennon**: Phil, I'm gonna write your history, so be careful.[4]

John was obviously messing with Spector, but there's an irony to his words: Elton John did suffer bouts of depression, and even made one attempt to kill himself,[5] though, at this point, he has made it to nearly seventy. More ironic, Phil Spector went to prison for murder.[6] This was history John Lennon didn't live to see.

That said, we can sometimes guess the future with the accuracy of a weatherman, but only God can perfectly predict it. It is proof that He is God.

Because of this, we have no excuse for rejecting the Bible. Those who do so because they are offended by the judgments of God or they believe Scripture is full of contradictions, have never humbly searched the Scriptures to see the uniqueness of this amazing Book, especially in the area of prophecy.

It is human nature to think that death is something that happens to *other* people. We somehow think that we are immortal, or at least we put it off as something that will come so far into the future, we needn't be concerned. John was no different. He thought he would live to be in his nineties. The *very* day he was murdered, he said, "I consider that my work won't be finished until I'm dead and buried, and I hope that's a long, long time."[7]

Notice again the opening verses of Psalm 90. Tucked within them, it says, "You turn man to destruction, and say, 'Return, O children of men'" (v. 3). This is a reference to the Fall of Genesis. When Adam and Eve sinned, they brought sin into the human race; they turned man to destruction. We each inherit a sinful nature, and because of our many sins, each of us attracts the just anger of God, like an irresistible magnet, to ourselves. Look at how the Bible speaks of God's anger abiding on us:

You carry them away like a flood; they are like a sleep. In the morning they are like grass which grows up: in the morning it flourishes and grows up; in the evening it is cut down and withers. For we have been consumed by Your anger, and by Your wrath we are terrified. You have set our iniquities before You, our secret sins in the light of Your countenance. For all our days have passed away in Your wrath; we finish our years like a sigh. The days of our lives are seventy years; and if by reason of strength they are eighty years, yet their boast is only labor and sorrow; for it is soon cut off, and we fly away. Who knows the power of Your anger? For as the fear of You, so is Your wrath. So teach us to number our days, that we may gain a heart of wisdom. (Psalm 90:5–12)[8]

God is not the beneficent butler most imagine Him to be, waiting on the needs and wants of mankind. Rather, He is a good and righteous Judge, and you and I are criminals who have greatly offended Him by our many transgressions. The thought that we are offensive to Him is offensive to many, so before we look at *our* many transgressions, let's look at those of another. John Lennon.

THE SINS OF JOHN LENNON

I'd like to live to a ripe old age, with Yoko only,
you know. And I'm not afraid of dying. I don't
know how it'd feel at the moment. But I'm
prepared for death because I don't believe in it.
I think it's just getting out of one car and getting
into another.[1]

~ *John Lennon*

WHEN JOHN WAS A YOUNG KID, he shoplifted, lied "about everything," drew dirty pictures, and ignored authority. He was the leader of the bad kids on the block. Rock and roll represented everything for which he lived.

John said of his youth that he was "a weird, psychotic kid covering up my insecurity with a macho facade."[2]

Speaking of his adultery later in life, he said, "Intellectually we knew marriage was a stupid scene, but we're romantic and square, as well as hip and aware. We lived together for a year before we got married, but we were still tied to other people by a bit of paper."[3] He and Yoko Ono were married in 1969, but a little later, John spent eighteen months with May Pang, who was their common secretary. He also had a relationship with the wife of the Beatles' road manager, Mal Evans.[4]

He began consuming LSD in 1964, and "it went on for years," he said. "I must have had a thousand trips . . . a thousand. I used it all the time."[5] He also admitted, "I have always needed a drug to survive. The others, too, but I always had more, more pills, more of everything because I am more crazy, probably."[6] Lennon said, "God isn't in a pill, but LSD explained the mystery of life," and in an interview with *Playboy*, he said that the Beatles smoked marijuana for breakfast.[7] In 1967, they placed one full-page ad in the *London Times*, requesting the legalization of marijuana. Later, in 1969, John said, "If people can't face up to the fact of other people being naked or smoking pot . . . then we're never going to get anywhere."[8]

But drugs weren't John's only vice. He also dabbled in the paranormal. John and Yoko owned a large selection of occult books,[9] and in 1974, Yoko hired John Green, an occultist, to be her tarot card reader. Green also "became Lennon's advisor, confidant, and friend. Until October of 1980, he worked closely with them. They did everything according to 'the cards.' He advised them on all of their business transactions and investments, even to the point of how to handle the problems Lennon was having with Apple, The Beatles['] record company."[10] "People were hired and fired based on the findings of the tarot card reader, Charlie Swan; the Council of Seers, an assortment of freelance astrologers, psychics and directionalists; and Yoko's own consultations with the zodiac and Book of Numbers."[11]

At one point, Yoko spent a week in Colombia, in South America, with a witch, learning how to cast spells. She paid the witch sixty thousand dollars. "The Lennons saw magic as both an instrument of crisis management and the ideal weapon."[12] They cast spells on their opponents during lawsuits, and also against Paul and Linda on one occasion.[13] Yoko combined numerology with cartography; this is an Asian philosophy known as *katu-tugai*. John and Yoko participated in séances, and she believed herself to be the reincarnation of a

Persian mummy dated three thousand years old, which she purchased in Switzerland.[14] Yoko also collected Egyptian things because she thought they had magical powers, and John wanted to find the spear used to pierce Jesus' side because he was certain that with it, he could do anything in the universe.[15]

Prone to losing his temper often and very easily, the man who sang "All You Need Is Love" and "Give Peace a Chance" was, in fact, very inconsistent. John's biographers mention "the infamous Lennon temper," and John himself agreed: "I was a hitter. I couldn't express myself, and I hit. I fought men, and I beat women."[16]

For example, once, when John thought that May Pang was cheating on him, he "flew into a rage, trashing the room and trampling her eyeglasses."[17] "I was a very jealous, possessive guy," he said. "A very insecure male. A guy who wants to put his woman in a little box and only bring her out when he feels like playing with her."[18]

He also told a friend, "I've always wondered what it would be like to kill a woman, many women! It was only becoming a Beatle that saved me from actually doing it."[19]

When Yoko was pregnant with Sean, their son, who was born in 1975, John kicked her in the stomach during a dispute. Years later, at a restaurant, he kicked Sean, too.[20]

Especially toward the end of his life, John needed psychological help, so he attended the Primal Institute in California, where Dr. Arthur Janov said, "John was simply not functioning. He really needed help."[21] He suffered from paranoia, and, once in 1976, while traveling to Hong Kong, he stayed in his suite for three days. He also thought his various personalities talked to him, and according to biographer Geoffrey Giuliano, "Lennon was in such a state of mind that the slightest noise or shadow would terrify him."[22]

In 1978, he "locked himself into his pristine, white-bricked, white-carpeted Dakota bedroom. Lying on the bed, he chain-smoked Gitane cigarettes and stared blankly at his giant television, while the muted phone at his side was lit by calls he never took. . . . He stayed in a dark room with the curtains drawn."[23] And by 1979, at the age of thirty-nine, "John Lennon was acting like an old man, haunted by his past and frightened by the future."[24]

That same year, Yoko convinced him to spend some time on their farm in Virginia, but after traveling back to New York by train, he "erupted violently, reducing the apartment to a shambles." The leader of the Beatles had "all but lost his creative drive and confessed he'd sunk so low he had even become terrified of composing."[25]

So John Lennon was no stranger to sin and its frightening consequences. He was a liar, a thief, a blasphemer, a fornicator, and an adulterer. In other words, he was no different from most of us. He was just a high-profile, average, red-blooded male, whose life was an offense to God.

Now that we have exposed someone else's sins, let's turn the spotlight back on ourselves for a moment, to make an important point.

In Scripture, a Christian is called a "believer." Yet, before my conversion, I *believed* in God. I *believed* that Jesus was the Son of God, and I *believed* that He rose from the dead. But I was not a believer in the biblical sense. This is because a true believer is someone who has trusted Jesus for his or her eternal salvation. I hadn't taken that step of faith. A skydiver can't rightly be called a skydiver until he takes a leap of faith out of the plane, and a sinner can't be called a believer until he entirely puts his faith in Jesus Christ, through the new birth.

Similarly, an unbeliever is called an "unbeliever," not necessarily because he doesn't believe in the existence of God, but because he lacks "saving" faith. He lives in what the Bible calls the "natural" world (1

Corinthians 2:14). He is like a man who was born blind reading a braille book titled *Amazing Color!* As he runs his fingers over the raised lettering, he whispers the words he is reading: "The sky is a beautiful blue. Luscious green grass fills the landscape as far as the eye can see. Two color-filled gardens are planted, one on each side of the grassy area. On one side, bright yellow flowers burst with wonderful color, and on the other side, vivid red roses explode with amazing energy, each one cupped in a cradle of wonderfully intense green leaves. The recent refreshing rain has left drops on the plants, sending streams of white light in different directions. A stunning rainbow, with its amazing seven colors of red, orange, yellow, green, blue, indigo, and violet, arches in all its glory across the massive blue heavens."

The blind man closes the book and thinks, *This makes no sense! I believe in science. I believe in logic and what can be proven, not in this thing called "color." I don't believe it exists, and anyone who does is a fool.*

He is right. His world does lack any semblance of color, so what could you say to such a closed-minded man? You could tell him that color exists, no matter what he does or doesn't believe about it. Reality isn't dictated by his belief. Then you could explain what color looks like. But how would you describe "blue" or "red"? You can't say that blue "looks like" anything because the blind man doesn't have anything in his mind to which he can compare it. What he needs is something you *can't* give him. He needs light, and that would take a miracle.

The Bible says that the unbeliever is blind. He is enclosed in his own "natural" worldview. He *cannot* see and he will often mock any thought of another dimension: "The natural man does not receive the things of the Spirit of God, for they are foolishness to him; nor can he know them, because they are spiritually discerned" (1 Corinthians 2:14). Therefore, unbelievers are "alienated from the life of God, because of the ignorance that is in them, because of the blindness of their heart" (Ephesians 4:18). And there's nothing you can do to help them see, if they are not willing to be honest. Every unbeliever needs the "light"; that is, the Word of God: "For the commandment is a lamp; and the law a light; reproofs of instruction are the way of life" (Proverbs 6:23). Unfortunately, "the god of this world hath blinded the minds of them which believe not, lest the light of the glorious gospel of Christ, who is the image of God, should shine unto them" (2 Corinthians 4:4 KJV). But if the unbeliever is prepared to look at the Ten Commandments with an honest heart, they will illuminate his need and help him understand the light of Christ's "glorious gospel." Jesus is the One who said, "I am the light of the world. He who follows Me shall not walk in darkness, but have the light of life" (John 8:12). There's the miracle.

As a Christian, I know that I have everlasting life, and so does every other person who has truly been born again. Death isn't the end for any Christian. It's the beginning. The knowledge that death has no sting is a wonderful, twenty-four-hour-a-day consolation. Of course, I am not excited about the way I will die, or the fact that I will leave those I love, but the mystery of it is gone, and so is the terror that comes with the unknown.

One kind lady recently wrote to me and said she was saving up so that she could fly to my funeral. She knows that it will be a great time of celebration. I have recorded a video clip to be aired at my funeral so that I can say something to those who come. I don't have some sort of weird death wish, but I do know that the day will come, and I can handle that.

Ten natives and a missionary were secretly flown out of war-torn Africa in the darkness of night. If they hadn't left immediately, rival tribes would have killed them. It was difficult for the missionary to coax the natives onto the plane because they had never even seen an aircraft before, let alone been on a flight.

Once they were in the air, the missionary found himself in a terrible dilemma. The plane was quickly running out of fuel, and was about to crash. He had five minutes to tell the men that each of them had to put on a parachute. He put his on and explained that he was going to jump ten thousand feet down to the safety of the ground, and that they must do the same. He then told them that if they stayed on the plane, they would die. They had to put on their parachutes. But for some unknown reason, they refused to follow his example. As the plane began to splutter, they sat there, terrified at their impending death.

How would you describe the missionary's mindset? First, he is not fearful to jump out into the darkness of the night, because he has complete faith in the parachute. It will save him. He knows that gravity will no longer pull him down to the earth at 120 miles per hour and break every bone in his body. His consolation in having a chute is inexpressible.

But at the same time, he is horrified at the fate of the ten men. If they don't put on the parachutes, they each will die a terrifying death. All they have to do to be saved is put on the chutes! That's the tragedy. It's then that the missionary finds out why they refuse to don their parachutes. They don't want to put them on because they think they will look foolish.

The Bible says, "Put on the Lord Jesus Christ" (Romans 13:14). Sadly, it also says, "The wicked one in the pride of his countenance will not seek, inquire for, and yearn for God; all his thoughts are that there is no God [so He never punishes]" (Psalm 10:4 AMP).

Late in 2010, I mentioned to my doctor that every now and then, food would sit for a short time in my esophagus. He was concerned and sent me to a specialist, who made an appointment for what I thought would be a simple exploratory procedure in which he would simply look down my throat with a special instrument.

I was very wrong. It was a full-scale operation. Before I knew it, I was prepped, put on a gurney, and wheeled into an operating room. I had tubes in my arm, oxygen in my nose, drugs in my system, and I was wired up to high-tech machines that were sending out beeping noises.

As I lay on the table, surrounded by nurses, I had a thought. I had been on more than a thousand flights, and had made a mischievous habit of making a *BONG!* noise after the incoming plane stopped at the terminal. I had learned to time it just before the authentic bong, which told passengers they could get their baggage, sounded, and I took great delight in seeing passengers stand up upon hearing the fake sound.

As I lay on the operating table, listening to the heart monitor, I was sorely tempted to do a "flatline" sound. I was sure I could do it without opening my eyes or my lips. It would just be a matter of getting the right key, and that would be easy. Fortunately, I resisted the temptation, because I imagined them grabbing those paddle things and shocking my healthy heart, which probably would have killed me. Defibrillators can give up to 2,500 volts.[26]

But if we are going to "shock" the non-Christian into reality, we must apply the two tablets of God's Law, like a defibrillator, to his heart. What we are talking about when it comes to where unbelievers will spend eternity is more serious than a heart attack.

And what about *you*? If you believe that you have sinned against God, you are what is known as a "wakened" sinner. But you must move from there to become an "anxious" sinner. Instead of just saying, "Okay, I see that I have sinned against God," you must come to a point of dread and cry, *"What must I do to be saved?"* Unless that happens, you will merely acknowledge your sinfulness, not find a place of true repentance, and either remain unconverted, or have a false conversion. So please take to heart what I'm saying. I wish John Lennon had.

THE MURDER OF
JOHN LENNON

I'll be 40 when this interview comes out. Paul is 38.
Elton John, Bob Dylan—we're all relatively young
people. The game isn't over yet. Everyone talks in
terms of the last record or the last Beatle concert—
but, God willing, there are another 40 years of
productivity to go. . . . I don't want to die at 40.[1]

~ *John Lennon*

O N   T H E   M O R N I N G   of December 8, 1980,
photographer Annie Leibovitz visited John
and Yoko's apartment, to do a photoshoot
for *Rolling Stone* magazine. Leibovitz had promised
that the couple's photo would make the cover, but on

that day, she wanted to photograph John without his wife. After the session, John gave his last interview to Dave Sholin, a DJ from San Francisco who had a music show on RKO Radio Network. Later, at 5 p.m., the couple left their apartment building to go to the Record Plant Studio to mix a song called "Walking on Thin Ice," sung by Yoko, with John on the lead guitar.

Mark David Chapman was a twenty-five-year-old security guard from Honolulu, Hawaii. That morning, he was among a group of fans that approached the limousine in which Yoko and John would be riding. Fans would often wait outside the Dakota building, seeking John's autograph. Approximately two months earlier, in October, Chapman had traveled to New York with the intention of murdering John, but he changed his mind at the last moment. He had even approached the ex-Beatle and asked for his autograph. Handing Chapman the signed album, Lennon asked, "Is this all you want?" Chapman nodded, and photographer Paul Goresh took a picture of that very moment.[2]

Several hours later, John and Yoko left the recording studio and returned to their apartment. John wanted to say good night to their son, Sean, who was just five, but he also liked to please the fans that had been waiting for him, by signing autographs and taking photos with them.

On this day, for some reason, John and Yoko didn't drive into the courtyard of their building, which was more secure, but instead left the limousine on Seventy-Second Street. If the limo had been driven inside, it would have prevented Chapman from killing John Lennon.

The Dakota's doorman, Jose Perdomo, and a taxi driver testified later that they saw Chapman waiting for John. Yoko walked ahead of her husband into the reception area. John looked at Chapman as he passed by, then Chapman shot five hollow-point bullets directly at John's back. One of the bullets passed over John's head into a window, two others hit him in the left side of his back, and the remaining two hit his left shoulder. But the very first shot pierced John's aorta. Chapman had used a Charter Arms .38 Special Revolver.

Most believed that Chapman dropped his gun immediately after he fired the shots, but he argued that he was actually tackled by the doorman. "I didn't drop it. I stood there and held it in my hand," he said. "And the doorman, Jose, came over and he said, 'What have you done, what have you done?' He grabbed my hand and he shook it, and he shook the weapon out of my hand, and he kicked it across the asphalt about thirty feet away. Pretty brave man to do that. But that's what he did." Chapman also remembered that after his arrest, Yoko walked up to the police car in which he was sitting and looked at him, but she didn't say a word.[3]

Chapman said later, "There was no emotion in my blood. There was no anger. There was nothing. It was dead silence in my brain. Dead, cold quiet, until he walked up. He looked at me . . . He walked past me and then I heard in my head. It said, 'Do it, do it, do it,' over and over again."[4]

Some newspaper, television, and radio reports said that just before he shot, Chapman called out, "Mr. Lennon" and dropped into a "combat stance,"[5] but this isn't stated in the court hearings or witness interviews. Chapman himself said he didn't remember saying John's name before shooting.

After the bullets entered his body, John took five steps into the reception area, and quietly said, "I'm shot!" Then he collapsed. The building's concierge covered John with his uniform, removed his blood-stained glasses, and called the police.

While waiting for police to arrive, Chapman removed his hat and coat and sat down on the sidewalk. Perdomo screamed at him, "DO YOU KNOW WHAT YOU'VE DONE?"

Chapman answered, "Yes, I just shot John Lennon."

When officers Peter Cullen and Steve Spiro arrived at the Dakota, they found Chapman already disarmed and sitting on the sidewalk "very calmly," carrying only a copy of J. D. Salinger's *The Catcher in the Rye*. He had written on the inside cover: "*To Holden Caulfield. From Holden Caulfield. This is my statement.*" Holden Caulfield was the book's main character, and Chapman later said that his life mirrored Caulfield's.

A second team of officers, Bill Gamble and James Moran, arrived and took Lennon into their car and rushed him to Roosevelt Hospital. En route, Officer Moran asked him, "Do you know who you are?" John nodded and tried to answer, but then he lost consciousness.

John Lennon had no pulse and wasn't breathing when Dr. Stephan Lynn received him in the emergency room. The damage in the aorta and vessels around the heart was so great that efforts to resuscitate him over twenty minutes were useless. By 11:07 p.m., some accounts say, Lennon had lost more than 80 percent of his blood and was pronounced dead at that time. Other reports say that Dr. Lynn pronounced him dead on arrival in the emergency room at 11:15 p.m. The official cause of death was listed as hypovolemic shock.

According to chief medical examiner, Dr. Elliot M. Gross, nobody could live for more than a few minutes with the type of wounds that John Lennon sustained. Hollow-point bullets expand once they hit a target, so John's tissue and organs were virtually destroyed by the bullets.[6]

Yoko was taken to Roosevelt Hospital, but was soon led away, in shock, by a friend. Hearing that her husband was dead, she sobbed "Oh no, no, no, no . . . tell me it's not true."

The next day, Yoko stated, "There is no funeral for John. John loved and prayed for the human race. Please do the same for him. Love, Yoko and Sean."[7]

The man who had wanted to give peace a chance, who had said, "But when you talk about destruction, don't you know you can count me out," tragically and ironically died a terrible and violent death. This was the same man who had once said:

> It's better to fade away like an old soldier than to burn out. I don't appreciate worship of dead Sid Vicious or of dead James Dean or of dead John Wayne. It's the same thing. Making Sid Vicious a hero, Jim Morrison—it's garbage to me. I worship the people who survive. Gloria Swanson, Greta Garbo. They're saying John Wayne conquered

cancer—he whipped it like a man. You know, I'm
sorry that he died and all that—I'm sorry for his
family—but he didn't whip cancer. It whipped him.
I don't want Sean worshiping John Wayne or Sid
Vicious. What do they teach you? Nothing. Death.
Sid Vicious died for what? So that we might rock?
I mean, it's garbage, you know. If Neil Young
admires that sentiment so much, why doesn't he
do it? Because he sure as hell faded away and came
back many times, like all of us. No, thank you. I'll
take the living and the healthy.[8]

We live in a society that has forgotten the
meaning of justice. The word has been twisted by
contemporary society from meaning "the administration of deserved punishment" to meaning "rehabilita-
tion." A prison is no longer a place of punishment for
guilty criminals, but a "correctional" facility. Take,
for instance, the killer of John Lennon, Mark David
Chapman. He came up for possible parole for the
sixth time, back in 2010, just months before the thir-
tieth anniversary of the former Beatle's death:

Chapman, 55, is serving a sentence of 20 years
to life in prison for the shooting death of Lennon
outside Lennon's New York City apartment on
December 8, 1980. He has served 29 years of his
sentence at the maximum-security Attica Correctional Facility, where he is held in a building
with other prisoners who are not considered to

> pose a threat to him, according to officials with the state Department of Correctional Services. He has his own prison cell but spends most of his day outside the cell working on housekeeping and in the library, the officials said. For the past 20 years, he has been allowed conjugal visits with his wife, Gloria. The visits are part of a state program called "family reunion" that allows inmates to spend up to 44 hours at a time with family members in a special setting. Inmates must meet certain criteria to receive the privilege.[9]

I have always been of the impression that if a man shot another man in the back, he was a coward. Chapman, like Hitler[10] and millions of others throughout history, professed to be a Christian,[11] but proved to be just another hypocrite—a pretender, a Judas, who betrayed the kindness Lennon showed to him by putting four bullets—two to the back and two to the shoulder—into his body.

The coward murdered him as he was on his way to see his beloved child and wife.

So how is this self-confessed murderer, whose hands drip with the blood of an unsuspecting man, being punished? He is given free meals, a warm bed, the security of a steady job in a bad economy, and regular sex . . . all for shooting John Lennon in the back.

JOHN'S DILEMMA

*J*OHN LENNON believed in Jesus, but he wasn't convinced of His exclusivity. Like millions of others, he understandably had difficulty with the thought that Jesus was the *only* way to God.

In spite of his flaws, John was an extremely loving man, and he genuinely believed in the power of love. It was the answer to human ills. Love is, indeed, "all you need."[1] Those who truly love, don't lie, steal, or kill. Real love would mean the end to all wars. It sounds too simple, but it is true.

John was a dreamer, but he wasn't the only one.

Today, as then, many have great difficulty with the thought that there is only *one way* to God. If *God* is love, these people say, He should allow many ways to get to heaven. To say that Jesus is the only way to heaven is to say that all Hindus, Buddhists, Muslims, and so forth, are not going to make it, and the only ones who are going there are narrow-minded Christians. The thought is ludicrous. But more than that, it's intolerant and it's hypocritical, because Christians are no better than anyone else. In fact, many Hindus are more holy and even better morally than Christians. And it's not just Hindus who are good. There are *millions* of really good, genuine, sincere people.

That seems to make sense, yet those who believe it is true will eventually find themselves in a quandary.

On January 14, 2007, a package was sent to the U.S. Holocaust Memorial Museum. It contained 116 personal photographs from a scrapbook that formerly belonged to a man named Karl Hoecker, first lieutenant to Richard Baer, who was the commandant of the infamous Auschwitz Nazi death camp. A documentary was made about the photographs.

The scrapbook showed, among other things, commandants of concentration camps, relaxing in their spare time. They were obviously winding down after a hard day at the office. They killed Jews during the day, and partied to get rid of any stress at night.

Sara J. Bloomfield, the director of the U.S. Holocaust Memorial Museum, on seeing the photos, said, "I think the big question about the holocaust is 'why?' Why do people kill? Why were so many people able to do this, in the heart of such a civilized nation? And it shows the killers as *humans*. This is a question that I think doesn't have answers."[2]

That's the dilemma each of us will face if we ignore the biblical revelation of the nature of human beings (see Colossians 3:5), and instead embrace the misguided notion that man is basically good. It will also be compounded by a Genesis-less worldview.

The Bible says that we live in a fallen world. It was created perfect by God in the beginning. But now, because of the Adamic Fall, we have disease, suffering, and death. When Adam sinned, he polluted his offspring with an evil nature—something the Bible calls "sin."

Embracing God's perspective immediately makes life make sense. When I read stories of the Holocaust and see horrific pictures that make me weep, I don't have the dilemma of wondering how human beings could do such a thing. What I see simply confirms what I have read—that sin dwells in every human heart. (See Matthew 15:19; Mark 7:21–22; Jeremiah 17:9.)

Sin not only makes us *capable* of evil; its very presence makes *us* evil. Evil isn't just something I do. According to the Bible, it is something I am. I am sinful—literally *full* of sin—by nature. (See Ephesians 2:3; Psalm 51:5.) Sin is as much a part of me as is my blood. This thought is extremely offensive to us—especially if we are convinced of the opposite, that humans are basically good. We want to think that humankind is good, not evil, because we want to think that *we*, individually, are good, not evil. But if we stay with that belief, we will be pushed into an intellectual corner, from which we have no escape.

However, when I look at life with the biblical perception, and ask how 200,000 people could be murdered in the United States during the 1990s, I don't have to say that each of those murderers was a good person who somehow strayed from his goodness. Instead, I affirm what the Scriptures say about the reality of sin in the human heart. When a husband beats his wife, a man shoots his children, the Mexican cartel beheads innocent people, a spouse betrays marital trust and commits adultery—all this does is verify the presence of sin.

When an atheist denies that God exists and uses His name to cuss, or when evil men deny the existence of evil, or when a man has an explosive temper he can't control or is consumed by bitterness, or when filthy or blasphemous language pours from a teenager's lips, or when I feel the power of lust or selfishness in my own heart, it just confirms the truth of Scripture. Today, pornography is a billion-dollar industry, priests are pedophiles, filthy and violent entertainment is loved by millions—and I know why. When kids are bullied or when people are racially prejudiced, I think "sin," not "skin."

Hypocrisy and double standards abound in politics and in the Church; kids kill kids at school; doctors kill children in the womb to make money; and slick televangelists use Christianity to line their pockets. Men use religion to kill others—they fly planes into buildings and torture people in the name of God, just as Catholics did during the Inquisition and Hitler did to the Jews. And each time I see it, I say, "Sin dwells in the human heart."

And when a professing Christian puts four bullets into the back of another human being, and does so because he wants to be famous, there's no mystery. There's no need to psychoanalyze him and try to find out what he has in common with other psychopaths. He's a normal human being. That's it. He's like the Nazis, the rapists, the pedophiles, the thieves and liars—or the "nice guy" who reads *Playboy*, the faithful husband who cheats on his income tax, or the doting father of four who cheats on his wife. He's like the man next door. His evil actions simply confirm that God's testimony about the human race is true and right.

The enigma of human suffering is also solved by believing the Bible. When tornadoes, hurricanes, and terrible diseases kill masses of people; lightning burns or kills; snakes bite; earthquakes or landslides take human life; or death takes our loved ones, it proves one thing: we live in a fallen, sinful creation, and "the wages of sin is death" (Romans 6:23).

So believing in Genesis has a calming effect on the human mind. There's no panic. There's no dilemma. But it also brings with it a frightening moral implication. The book of Genesis isn't alone. It is married to Exodus, and there are sixty-four other members of the family. The Bible isn't just one book. It's a total of sixty-six books, and its harmonizing message is that we are sinful, wicked, fallen, and that we are responsible for our actions. Exodus points out our sins, and it stands as an accusing prosecutor, demanding the death sentence. (See Romans 6:23.)

Another commentator during the Nazi documentary was Michael Berenbaum, PhD. He was the director of the Zeiring Holocaust Institute. Mr. Berenbaum was intelligent and thoughtful as he spoke about the smiling officers who cruelly killed so many Jews. He said, "We would like to believe that there is a God who metes out justice in this world . . . It makes us wish that there is a world after this world, in which justice is meet out at evil."[3]

Of course, we would like to believe that there is a God who is going to punish those who murdered the Jews. It would also be nice to believe there is a God who is going to punish those who murdered Gentiles as well. Here, now, is what is going to sound like a huge oxymoron, but it's not: the good news of the Bible is that *hell exists.*

But hell isn't just for Nazis. It's for the murderous mafia, the Mexican cartel, for Islamic terrorists, for mass murderers, for one-time murderers, for those who *wanted* to murder, for rapists, thieves, liars, fornicators, adulterers, for the lustful, the greedy, the jealous, for blasphemers, and for the unthankful. Suddenly, hell doesn't seem like such a good idea. It's no longer good news because it's no longer me who is standing as a righteous judge pointing at the evil Nazis. The moral law of God points its perfect finger at me, and proclaims me not only guilty, but evil by nature, and requires death, and then damnation.

So not only does man find himself in a fallen creation, with a sinful heart, but he can't redeem himself either. He can't do anything to acquit himself from the courtroom of Eternal Justice. What can we say—"I'm really a good person"? That's just not true, from God's perspective. Without the knowledge that the moral law brings, you and I will *think* we are basically good, and that we can merit God's favor and earn everlasting life by our good works. But more than that, any talk of the exclusivity of Jesus Christ will seem intolerant and unloving and could even be considered by the politically correct as "hate speech." The thought that He is the only way to find everlasting life will be seen by us as nothing but religious extremism.

On August 5, 2010, part of the San José copper–gold mine in the Atacama Desert near Copiapó, Chile, collapsed, leaving thirty-three men trapped 2,300 feet under ground. However, all thirty-three miners were safely rescued and brought to the surface sixty-nine days later, on October 13, through a narrow hole that had been drilled down to reach them.

It was estimated that more than a billion people watched the rescue on live television around the world. Each of the men had to be winched in a rescue capsule, reaching the surface in sixteen minutes. The total cost of the rescue operation was around $20 million (US).

Can you imagine being one of those men, hopelessly trapped deeper than 2,300 feet under the ground? They could move around, and they had limited food and water, but it was just a matter of time until they died in the darkness, in a mass grave.

But hope came from above. Compassionate rescuers spent millions of dollars and went to great effort to drill one narrow way down to them, so they could be brought back from the very brink of a sure death. When the offer of rescue came, every single miner gladly climbed into that narrow capsule and did exactly as he was instructed by the rescuers. Not one of them said, "I am offended that there is only one way out of here. I don't like this narrow way, and anyone who offers it is narrow-minded. Instead, I am going to dig my own way out, thank you!"

Anyone who would say something like that would have to be insane!

Yet such is the way of those who are offended by what God did to rescue hopeless sinners from a sure death. Until God gives us light through the gospel, we sit helplessly in the black shadow of death. We can move around, and we have food and drink, but we are trapped, waiting to die. It's just a matter of time. Yet rescue came from above. God Himself is rich in mercy and didn't leave us alone in our darkness. He made a way for us to be rescued, and it didn't cost a mere $20 million. It cost the precious blood of His Son, who suffered agony on the cross of Calvary. God said through the prophets that He would rescue us from the grave, and that there would be only one way of salvation. (See Isaiah 49 and Jeremiah 32:39.) He then became a Man in the person of Jesus of Nazareth and bore the punishment for the sin of the world, so we could come out of the darkness into the glorious light, out of sure death into everlasting life.

There is only one way to be saved, and it's straight and it's narrow (Matthew 7:14; John 14:6). Obey the gospel and be rescued from the power of the grave. Please, oh, please, don't insist on trying to dig your way out of this mess. Repent of your sins, and trust alone in the Savior: "Nor is there salvation in any other, for there is no other name under heaven given among men by which we must be saved" (Acts 4:12).

John Lennon said, "You've got to get down to your own God in your own temple. It's all down to you, mate."[4] Not according to the Word of God.

· 8 ·

JOHN'S BAD RAP

My defenses were so great. The cocky rock and
roll hero who knows all the answers was actually a
terrified guy who didn't know how to cry. Simple.[1]

~ *John Lennon*

*I*BELIEVE THAT HISTORY has given
John Lennon a bad rap. Like all of us, he had
his many sins, but he wasn't the hard, satani-
cally driven, proud, anti-Christian, God-hating person
many make him out to be. Still, after reading of his

87

life and death, some cold-hearted person seemed to sum up the attitude of many: "While this is a nice biography, I fail to see exactly what your point is. Radicals come and they go. Lennon wrote some nice music, but, really, other than that, what did he contribute? Finally, just because he wrote some nice music, so what, who cares? He . . . is dead. Can we move on now?"[2]

While traveling during their honeymoon, John and Yoko made their first Bed-In for Peace at the Hilton Hotel in Amsterdam. The local media mocked what they did, but John wasn't at all discouraged, and decided to try another one, this time in New York. However, authorities in New York blocked it, so the second Bed-In was held in Montreal in March 1969, and it attracted media from all around the world. The antiwar anthem "Give Peace a Chance" was recorded live at the Queen Elizabeth Hotel in Montreal. It was later sung by 250,000 anti–Vietnam War demonstrators on October 15, in Washington, D.C., when the second Vietnam Moratorium Day took place.

John and Yoko then moved to New York City in August 1971, where they met two radical antiwar activists, Jerry Rubin and Abbie Hoffman. At that time, John Sinclair, another activist, poet, and cofounder of the White Panther Party, was serving a ten-year sentence for selling two joints to an undercover police officer. On December 10, 1971, a "Free John Sinclair" concert was held in Ann Arbor, Michigan. The organizers convinced John and Yoko to come, and they shared the stage with other well-known artists, such as Stevie Wonder, David Peel, Phil Ochs, Bob Seger, and Bobby Seale of the Black Panther Party. John played his new song, "John Sinclair" in front of 20,000 people who were present at the rally. Three days later, the state of Michigan decided to set Sinclair free. Such was the power of John Lennon.

In 1972, the British army shot twenty-seven civil rights protestors during a march in Northern Ireland. That day became known as Bloody Sunday. John said that if he had a choice between the army and the IRA (Irish Republican Army), he would choose the latter. MI5 (the Security Service in the UK) revealed in the year 2000, that John had given money to the IRA. John and Yoko also supported, according to biographer Bill Harry, the production of *The Irish Tapes*, a pro-IRA documentary film.[3] According to the FBI, John was also sympathetic to Tariq Ali's International Marxist Group.[4]

Richard Nixon said, "When somebody in a show business comes and participates in a political rally, he or she is doing something that is a very great personal sacrifice, and even a personal risk."[5] It was around that time that the FBI began to monitor John Lennon. He maintained that they tapped his phone and followed him everywhere. He even began to suspect that some of his closest friends were working with the FBI. John said, "I think they wanted me to know [—] to scare me, and I was scared, paranoid."[6] His influence in the anti–Vietnam War protests, particularly with his song "Give Peace a Chance" was a threat to the Nixon administration. There were rumors that John wanted to appear in a concert in San Diego the same day as the Republican National Convention, and Nixon thought that John's antiwar initiatives could cost him his reelection.

John couldn't have cared less. He said:

> Our society is run by insane people for insane objectives. . . . If anybody can put on paper what our government, and the American government, and the Russian, Chinese . . . what they are actually trying to do, and what they think they're doing, I'd be very pleased to know what they think they're doing. I think they're all insane. But I am liable to be put away as insane for expressing that, that's what's insane about it.[7]

In February 1972, senator Strom Thurmond (R-SC) suggested in a memo that "deportation would be a strategic counter-measure" against John. The following month, the Immigration and Naturalization Service started the process to deport John, saying that his 1968 conviction in London for possession of cannabis had rendered him ineligible for admission to the nited States.[8]

John spent the next four years in deportation hearings and appearing on television programs, even cohosting *The Mike Douglas Show* for a week with Yoko. In the meantime, Bob Dylan wrote a letter to the INS, defending John. It read:

> John and Yoko add a great voice and drive to the country's so-called art institution. They inspire and transcend and stimulate and by doing so, only help others to see pure light and in doing that, put an end to this dull taste of petty commercialism which is being passed off as Artist Art by the overpowering mass media. Hurray for John and Yoko. Let them stay and live here and breathe. The country's got plenty of room and space. Let John and Yoko stay![9]

John was ordered to leave the United States on March 23, 1973. He was given sixty days to do so. John and Yoko responded with a press conference on April 1, 1973, announcing the creation of the state of "Nutopia," a place with "no land, no boundaries, no passports, only people."[10] They waved two handkerchiefs as their flags and asked for political asylum in the United States.

The Watergate hearings began soon after the press conference and fourteen months later, President Nixon resigned. Gerald Ford, his successor, didn't continue the battle against John and even overturned the deportation order in 1975. The following year, John Lennon received his green card.

When historian Jon Wiener requested the FBI files related to the deportation attempt, the FBI refused to release most of the documents, maintaining that they contained national security information. When the FBI admitted to having 281 pages of files on John Lennon, Wiener sued the FBI in 1983, not winning the suit until eight years later, in 1991. The Justice Department appealed the decision in April 1992, but the Supreme Court refused to review the case. By 1997, all but ten of the contested documents were released following President Bill Clinton's rule stating that files should be held only if releasing them would bring "foreseeable harm."[11]

Wiener published the results of those fourteen years in January 2000, in *Gimme Some Truth: The*

John Lennon FBI Files, which contained "lengthy reports by confidential informants detailing the daily lives of anti-war activists, memos to the White House, transcripts of TV shows on which Lennon appeared, and a proposal that Lennon be arrested by local police on drug charges." The other ten documents that were withheld, contain "national security information provided by a foreign government under an explicit promise of confidentiality."[12] Those files were released in December 2006 and showed no sign of the British government considering him as a threat.

John Lennon was offended at the hypocrisy of religion, and he was outspoken about his convictions about what he and millions saw as an unjust war. That's the side that most see. However, there was a tenderness about him of which many know nothing. Speaking of their differing personalities, this is what Paul McCartney said of John:

> "John's was more abrasive than mine and that was good for his corner of the square that made up the Beatles."
>
> [. . .]
>
> Sir Paul told the magazine that Lennon's image was "seriously flawed" because "he was not the hard, mad man that people think he was.

He was a very soft-centred guy and we had a lot more in common than people think," he said.

"His favourite song when we were kids was Little White Lies, which was very sentimental. It was a smoochy old standard that his mum liked.

Whatever bad things John said about me, he would also slip his glasses down to the end of his nose and say, "I love you'. That's really what I hold on to. That's what I believe. The rest is showing off."[13]

Scottish Bible teacher Alistair Begg said of John:

And when you read the biographies that have been done of Lennon, no matter who's writing them or what they're trying to say in them, one of the things that comes across is the fact of his almost embarrassing level of generosity. You know, he would . . . Someone would come over and say, My, that's a lovely thing, you know. And they would walk away with it. He bought his aunt a home. And he bought somebody a home. And there's a wonderful story that took place up in the north of Scotland that not many people know about.[14]

The interviewer then asked for details, to which Begg replied:

Well, he crashed his car up in Scotland soon after
he had married Yoko Ono. And as a result of that
he was hospitalized. They ran the car into a ditch.
And so here he is way in the—in the wilds of Scotland in a tiny, wee country hospital. And the local
minister comes to make his rounds. And in one
of the beds sits Lennon, you know, with his hair
way down his back. And the—the man, bless his
heart, duly goes up and introduces himself and
says who he is. And he actually, I believe, from
those who were part of this man's congregation,
had a wonderful opportunity to talk with him
beyond the level of superficial things. And a couple
of days later Lennon was stitched up and packed
off and he left. And within a week or ten days the
local minister was seen driving around the town in
this lovely new car. And apparently what had happened was that Lennon, when he was discharged
from the hospital, had gone to the local garage and
had written a check and asked the—the garage
owner to call the minister and offer to him any car
of his choice at Lennon's expense. And that was
an indication again of this heart.[15]

The problem was that millions of fans put the
Beatles, and particularly John, above an iconic status.
They were almost worshipped by an entire generation
of fans. This obviously frustrated him:

Why should The Beatles give more? Didn't they
give everything on God's earth for ten years?
Didn't they give themselves? You're like the

typical sort of love-hate fan who says, "Thank you for everything you did for us in the Sixties . . . would you just give me another shot? Just one more miracle?" . . .

If they didn't understand the Beatles and the Sixties then, what the f___ could we do for them now? Do we have to divide the fish and the loaves for the multitudes again? Do we have to get crucified again? Do we have to do the walking on water again because a whole pile of dummies didn't see it the first time, or didn't believe it when they saw it? You know, that's what they're asking: "Get off the cross. I didn't understand the first bit yet. Can you do that again?" No way. You can never go home. It doesn't exist.[16]

John Lennon was more than the leader of the Beatles. He was looked upon as a leader of a generation. But he was lost, and no doubt he felt uncomfortable leading when he knew he was lost. It was a role he didn't want. Look at his advice:

Produce your own dream. If you want to save Peru, go save Peru. It's quite possible to do anything, but not to put it on the leaders and the parking meters. Don't expect Jimmy Carter or Ronald Reagan or John Lennon or Yoko Ono or Bob Dylan or Jesus Christ to come and do it for you. You have to do it yourself. That's what the great masters and mistresses have been saying ever since time began. They can point the way, leave signposts and little instructions in various books that are now called holy and worshipped for the cover of the book and not for what it says, but the instructions are all there for all to see, have always been and always will be. There's nothing new under the sun. All the roads lead to Rome. And people cannot provide it for you. I can't wake you up. You can wake you up. I can't cure you. You can cure you.[17]

This quote reveals his lack of understanding as to who Jesus was. He lumped Him in with presidents and rock musicians. It's as though he wasn't really talking about presidents and musicians, but about our attitude toward Christianity: don't expect Jesus to do anything more for you than point the way for you to go somewhere yourself. It's as though John was speaking from his experience.

A few years earlier, in 1977, John made a profession of faith in Christ after being exposed to the world of televangelists. He would use expressions such as "Praise the Lord" and "Thank You, Jesus."[18] He even attended Christian churches several times and took Sean with him, trying to peak Yoko's interest in Christianity. He composed but never released a song called, "You Saved My Soul." But at the same time, John continued to participate in occult rituals, celebrate Buddha's birthday, and consult horoscopes and prognosticators.[19]

His interest in Christianity didn't last long. The moment he was confronted by a couple of missionaries with fundamental doctrines of the Bible, he turned back.[20]

Then, in 1979, he wrote "Serve Yourself," in which he said he ignored references to God and said that we have to serve ourselves.[21]

And finally, in 1980, the year of his death, he said he was "Zen Christian, Zen pagan, Zen Marxist" or nothing at all.[22]

JOHN LENNON'S MURDERER

I would listen to his music and I would get angry at
him, for saying that he didn't believe in God . . . and
that he didn't believe in Beatles.[1]

~ Mark Chapman

MARK DAVID CHAPMAN was born
on May 10, 1955, in Fort Worth, Texas.
His father was a sergeant in the U.S. Air
Force and his mother was a nurse.

As a child, Chapman imagined that he had a

group that he called "little people," over which he was a type of god. He was an abused child, terrified both of his father and of school bullies, who picked on him for his lack of sports skill. When that happened, he fell back on his imaginary friends. He told his biographer: "I used to fantasize that I was a king, and I had all these Little People around me and that they lived in the walls. And that I was their hero and was in the paper every day and I was on TV every day, their TV, and that I was important. They all kind of worshipped me, you know. It was like I could do no wrong."[2]

When he wanted to entertain his subjects, he would give them concerts, playing records. His favorite (and theirs), was the Beatles. Chapman recalls, "And sometimes when I'd get mad I'd blow some of them up. I'd have this push-button thing, part of the [sofa], and I'd like get mad and blow out part of the wall and a lot of them would die. But the people would still forgive me for that, and, you know, everything got back to normal. That's a fantasy I had for many years."[3]

Chapman attended Columbia High School in Decatur, Georgia, where he began using drugs when he was fourteen. He also skipped classes and once ran away to live in the streets for a couple of weeks, where he used marijuana, LSD, mescaline, heroine, and barbiturates. One of his friends said, "One thing about Mark, he didn't take [drugs] for recreation. He really believed in mind expansion. It was almost a kind of religious thing with him." He also believed in the Beatles, whose pictures covered his bedroom walls, particularly pictures of John Lennon.

At age sixteen, Chapman professed to become a Christian, regularly distributing gospel tracts and sharing his newfound faith. Newton Hendrix, who sang in school choir with Chapman, and went on to serve as music director of Fortified Hills Baptist Church in Smyrna, Georgia, said of this time, "I remember seeing him witnessing about Jesus to one of our classmates. That meant a lot to me. And now here he is stalking John Lennon and killing him? Is there something wrong with all of us?"[4]

Chapman also worked at a YMCA summer camp and was even made assistant director after winning an Outstanding Counselor award.[5]

One day, a friend recommended the book *The Catcher in the Rye* to Chapman. It so influenced him that he began to model his own life after that of the book's main character, Holden Caulfield.

Caulfield, who narrates his story in first person, is a lonely teenager, struggling in the transition from adolescence to adulthood as he tries to find his identity. He is deeply affected by the death of his brother and by a schoolmate's suicide after being bullied. At thirteen, after a violent emotional breakdown, he is taken to an asylum to be psychoanalyzed.

Considering adults to be corrupt, phony, and blinded by their phoniness, Holden doesn't want to become an adult. He criticizes their activities but has taken part in them by excessive drinking, smoking, flirting with older women, and going to nightclubs. Ultimately, Holden is alienated from society. The entire story is told from within the walls of an asylum.

The title represents the idea of a rye field at the edge of a cliff, upon which children played. The catcher, Holden, prevents the children from falling— from losing their innocence and becoming phony adults. The publication itself was banned from some school libraries because of the sexual content and its offensive language. There are 224 instances where obscene language is used.[6]

Chapman graduated from Columbia High School and moved to Chicago, where he joined his girlfriend to study at Covenant College, a Presbyterian institution, in Lookout Mountain, Georgia. There he became sexually involved with another woman and was so filled with guilt that he began to have suicidal thoughts. He broke up with his girlfriend, dropped out of college, and took a job as a security guard after qualifying to be an armed guard. His score on the pistol range was 80—the passing grade was 60.

Later, he tried to attend college again, but dropped out once more.

In 1977, Chapman attempted suicide while in Hawaii. Using a vacuum cleaner hose connected to his car's exhaust pipe, he breathed in carbon monoxide. The hose melted, and his attempt failed. Afterward, he was found, taken to a mental health clinic for treatment, diagnosed with clinical depression, and admitted at Castle Memorial Hospital. After his release, he was hired by the hospital, where he began to counsel other patients and play the guitar to them.

Chapman became further obsessed with *The Catcher in the Rye*, as well as with John Lennon and with music. He also began to hear voices, and in 1980, in a letter to his friend Lynda Irish, he stated, "I'm going nuts," signed, "The Catcher in the Rye."[7]

In 1978, he took a six-week trip around the world after being inspired by the film *Around the World in Eighty Days*. He visited Tokyo, Seoul, Hong Kong, Singapore, Bangkok, Delhi, Israel, Geneva, London, Paris, and Dublin. He then began a relationship with Gloria Abe—his travel agent, and on June 2, 1979, they were married. For a time, he worked as a printer at Castle Memorial Hospital, but soon he began to have problems, and he quit his job and started to drink heavily.

In October 1980, he visited New York, intending to murder John Lennon, but changed his mind and returned to Hawaii, where he told his wife of his obsession with assassinating Lennon.

He flew back to New York on December 6. Two days later, after leaving his hotel room, making sure to leave some items behind for police to find, he went to a local bookstore and bought a copy of *The Catcher in the Rye*, in which he wrote, "This is my statement," and signed it, "Holden Caulfield."[8]

THE MURDER

Later, Chapman showed up at John's residence, outside the Dakota building. As Chapman chatted with a photographer and the doorman of the Dakota, he showed them John Lennon's latest album that he had just bought.

At approximately 5 p.m., he saw John and Yoko coming out of the Dakota. They were on their way to a recording session. Chapman froze. The photographer, Goresh, had to push him closer to John Lennon, and without a word, Chapman handed the album and the pen to John. John smiled and signed "John Lennon, December 1980."

Chapman recounted the story on *Mugshots* ten years after the event:

> He said "Sure" and wrote his name, and when he handed it back to me he looked at me and kind of nodded his head, "Is that all you want?" Like just like that, like an inquiry into a different matter, and I said, "Yeah." I said, "Thanks, John." And he again said, "Is that all you want?" and there was Yoko; she was already in the car, the limo, the door was open and it was running, it was out in the middle of the street and he asked me twice, and I said, "Yeah, thanks, that's all," or something like that. He got into the car and drove away.[9]

Chapman remembered that as he took the album from John, a gun was in his pocket. After John departed, he said, "They're never going to believe this back in Hawaii," and offered fifty dollars to the photographer in exchange for a picture of him with Lennon. As the photographer started to leave, Chapman said, "I'd wait. You never know if you'll see him again."[10] The photographer left anyway, but not before Chapman could ask him to bring the photo to him the next day.

Further recalling the event, Chapman said, "I was just overwhelmed by [Lennon's] sincerity. I had expected a brush-off, but it was just the opposite. I was on Cloud Nine. And there was a little bit of me going, 'Why didn't you shoot him?' And I said, 'I can't shoot him like this. I wanted to get the autograph.'"

He also said that for the first time in a while, he prayed for strength to just take the signed album and go back home: "I remember I was praying to God [to keep me from killing Lennon] and I was also praying to the devil to give me the opportunity. 'Cause I knew I would not have the strength on my own."[11]

When the limousine returned from the recording session at 10:49 p.m., Chapman was still there. John and Yoko stepped out of the car and walked past Chapman, toward the entrance of their building. Chapman then drew a Charter Arms .38 firearm and shot five hollow-point bullets toward John's back. As stated earlier, one of those bullets pierced his aorta and caused massive bleeding.

Lennon struggled into the reception area, with Yoko screaming. Sean Strub, a witness, remembers: "I never saw anything like the look on her face. Her mouth was open wide like a whale's, her arms covering him like an animal. She looked as though she had been electrocuted."[12]

Meanwhile, Chapman was calm. When security screamed at him, asking if he knew what he had done, he replied, "I just shot John Lennon." He then took his copy of *The Catcher in the Rye* from his pocket and began reading coolly, as he waited for the police to arrive.

Three hours later, in his statement, Chapman said, "I am sure the large part of me is Holden Caulfield, who is the main person in the book. The small part of me must be the Devil." (He later sent a handwritten statement to the *New York Times*, saying that *Catcher* was "an extraordinary book that holds many answers," and that everybody should read it.)[13]

Chapman was charged with second-degree murder.

In January 1981, Jonathan Marks, Chapman's lawyer, pleaded not guilty due to insanity. The defense team was sure that Chapman would be found not guilty, and then be sent to a mental hospital to receive treatment. However, in June, Chapman told his lawyer that he wanted to plead guilty, and on June 22, Chapman said in a hearing that God had told him to plead guilty, and that he would not change his plea regardless of the sentence. Judge Dennis Edwards said that Chapman had decided of his own free will and that he thought he was competent to plead guilty.

The sentencing hearing took place on August 24, at which time, the District attorney said Chapman's crime was committed as an easy route to fame. When Chapman was asked if he had anything to say, he stood up and read a passage from *The Catcher in the Rye*:

> Anyway, I keep picturing all these little kids playing some game in this big field of rye and all. Thousands of little kids, and nobody's around—nobody big, I mean—except me. And I'm standing on the edge of some crazy cliff. What I have to do, I have to catch everybody if they start to go over the cliff—I mean if they're running and they don't look where they're going I have to come out from somewhere and catch them. That's all I do all day. I'd just be the catcher in the rye and all.[14]

The judge sentenced Chapman to twenty years to life in prison, as well as psychiatric treatment. (The maximum possible was twenty-five years to life.) He has been in the Attica Correctional Facility near Buffalo, New York, ever since.

Today Chapman is in the Security Housing Unit, a unit designed for violent and at-risk prisoners. He has his own cell but "spends most of his day outside his cell working on housekeeping and in the library."[15]

He works in the prison as a legal clerk and kitchen helper. He enjoys reading and writing short stories.

In 2004, he had a parole hearing, at which he stated that his plans, if released, would be to "immediately try to find a job, and I really want to go from place to place," he said, "at least in the state, church to church, and tell people what happened to me and point them the way to Christ." He also said that he wanted to set up a church with his wife.[16]

Chapman is part of the Family Reunion Program, which allows him to receive one conjugal visit a year with his wife. In addition to other visits from her, he can spend up to forty-two hours alone with her in a prison home. Occasionally, he also receives visits from his sister, friends, and ministers.[17]

A three-member board has denied him parole many times. In less than an hour following an October 2000 hearing, in which Chapman said he was sorry for the effect his crime had on Yoko Ono, the parole board concluded that releasing Chapman would "deprecate the seriousness of the crime and serve to undermine respect for the law."[18] Two years later, the parole board repeated their verdict. Even if his record inside prison was very positive, they said, they couldn't predict his behavior in the outside community.

Parole was denied a third time in October 2004,

when the board said their reason was based in part on Yoko's "monumental suffering by her witnessing the crime."[19] Also, around six thousand fans had signed an online petition, threatening vengeance if Chapman was released.

In a sixteen-minute parole hearing in 2006, the board concluded that it was better for Chapman and the community if he stayed in prison.

On the twenty-sixth anniversary of John's death, December 8, Yoko published a one-page advertisement in various newspapers, saying that December 8 should be a "day of forgiveness." However, she said she hadn't forgiven Chapman yet, and wasn't ready to.

For the fifth time, parole was denied on August 12, 2008, "due to concern for the public safety and welfare."[20]

In spite of Chapman's heinous crime, he was a big fan of the Beatles, and especially of John. The sister of one of his best friends confirmed that he had simply been angry at John's comments about Christ in 1966, when he said that the Beatles were more popular than Jesus. She said that Chapman "seemed really angry toward John Lennon, and he kept saying he could not understand why he had said it. He believed that nobody should be more popular than Jesus Christ. He said it was blasphemy."[21] Chapman's wife also said

The Beatles at St. George Hotel in Wellington, shortly after their arrival in New Zealand on June 21, 1964.

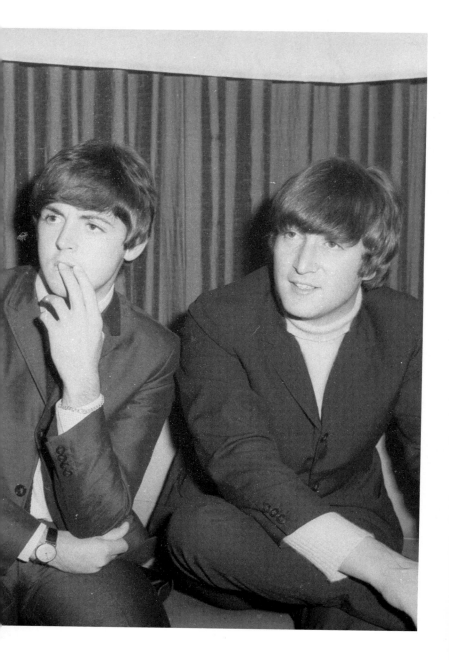

ABOVE AND RIGHT: Drummer, Ringo Starr.

OPPOSITE: Paul McCartney and John Lennon at the Sheraton Motor Hotel in Potts Point on June 11, 1964.

LEFT AND RIGHT: Ringo Starr and George Harrison.

John Lennon boarding a National Airways Corporation aircraft at
Wellington Airport in New Zealand.

The media with The Beatles shortly after their arrival in Wellington on June 21, 1964.

The Beatles with New Zealand's indigenous Maoris.

The Beatles at Wellington Airport during their New Zealand tour, June 1964.

LEFT: John Lennon with second cousins from New Zealand.
RIGHT: John Lennon with his second cousins: Mark, Susan, and Helen Parker (from left), June 23, 1964.

ABOVE: Paul McCartney, John Lennon, and George Harrison during their Wellington concert.

Ringo Starr and George Harrison greeted by New Zealand Maoris.

The Beatles arriving in Sydney, Australia on June 18, 1964.

that "he was angry that Lennon would preach love and peace but yet have millions [of dollars]."[22] Later, Chapman himself said, "[Lennon] told us to imagine no possessions, and there he was, with millions of dollars and yachts and farms and country estates, laughing at people like me who had believed the lies and bought the records and built a big part of their lives around his music."[23] Chapman remembers:

> I would listen to his music and I would get angry at him, for saying that he didn't believe in God and that he didn't believe in Beatles. This was another thing that angered me, even though this record had been done at least 10 years previously. I just wanted to scream out loud, "Who does he think he is, saying these things about God and heaven and The Beatles?" Saying that he doesn't believe in Jesus and things like that. At that point, my mind was going through a total blackness of anger and rage.[24]

When Chapman underwent psychiatric assessments, he described anger toward his father. He also identified himself with Dorothy from *The Wizard of Oz* and with Holden Caulfield, and talked about his chats with the imaginary "Little People," who used to direct him. He said they had begged him not to kill John Lennon. "Please, think of your wife. Please, Mr.

President. Think of your mother. Think of yourself," the voices had said. But Chapman told them he had already decided, so they became quiet.[25]

He also revealed a list of other celebrities he had thought of killing—and all of this while claiming to be a *Christian*.

MURDERER AND CHRISTIAN

Laurel and Hardy, that's John and Yoko. And we
stand a better chance under that guise because all
the serious people like Martin Luther King and
Kennedy and Gandhi got shot.[1]

~ John Lennon

MARK CHAPMAN was a believer in Jesus
Christ. In fact, he considered himself to
be a Christian. It happened during his
junior year at Columbia High School, according to
a former classmate: "One day this evangelist came

to a pep rally at the school and that night everybody went to a revival he staged and got saved."[2] Chapman, along with two hundred other children that day, had made a "decision for Christ."

I have devoted the last thirty years of my life exposing the damage done by these types of evangelists, whose message is far from accurate and complete. John Lennon's "conversion" that he had later in life was more than likely the result of the same erroneous message.

On the cover of my book on the subject, called *God Has a Wonderful Plan for Your Life: The Myth of the Modern Message*,[3] I contrasted the title with a picture of Stephen being stoned to death for his faith.[4] That's because I believe modern evangelists have intentionally distorted the gospel so they can get "decisions for Jesus." The Christian life is presented as a life-enhancement message: "God has a wonderful plan for your life. He will give you peace, joy, love, and fulfillment. He will fill the God-shaped hole in your heart and fix all your problems." But they neglect to tell you that eleven of the original twelve disciples were murdered for their faith. They also fail to say that when you become a Christian, you will be hated for your faith, and that Jesus Himself said that people will even kill you, thinking they are doing God a favor (John 16:2).

The fruit of modern evangelism's flawed message is the tragic life of Mark David Chapman. He was a false convert. So was Judas Iscariot. So are millions within the church today who live lives of hypocrisy rather than being genuine in their faith. Instead of hearing that they have violated the Ten Commandments and greatly offended God, they hear that God is like some sort of divine butler, whose supreme reason for existence is to run after the needs of those who invite Jesus into their hearts. So instead of repenting and surrendering to the Savior, these people give their hearts to Jesus in the hope of finding a better life—one without problems, filled with joy and harmony.

But that's not the real world, and it's not long until they are disillusioned. They are false converts—described in the Bible as goats among the sheep. And God will sort them out on Judgment Day. (See Acts 17:30, 31.)

After Chapman's decision for Christ, his life improved. He stopped taking drugs, and "for several months he preached and witnessed openly during school, antagonizing several old friends. He got a haircut, discarded his rumpled fatigue jacket, and began wearing a large, hand-crafted cross. He carried

a notebook inscribed JESUS, and turned vocifer-
ously against rock 'n' roll." Unfortunately, "in doing
so, the new Mark turned against John Lennon in
particular."[5]

Lennon's killer had all the classic signs of a false
convert.

The Bible teaches that you can tell a false convert
because his "roots" are shallow. Consequently, all the
goodness of the seed that should reach down into the
roots shoots instead up into the branches. A spurious
conversion will look impressive on the outside, just
like a quick-growing plant. But when the sun comes
out, the plant will wither and die because it has no
root depth. This is what Jesus said as He related the
difference between the genuine and the false in the
Parable of the Sower (see Mark 4). A well-meaning
but insincere convert may seem to "shoot up" quickly,
but the "sun," representing temptations and trials,
exposes the falseness of his conversion the first time
persecution comes his way.

Notice how Mark Chapman expressed his faith.
He wore a large wooden cross, and he carried a notebook with "JESUS" written on it. What he lacked
inwardly, he expressed to impress outwardly. To
the untrained eye, Mark Chapman was a zealous
Christian.

When Chapman appeared on CNN's *Larry King Live*, he was asked, "Did you have, prior to the conversion to the Lord, remorse?" Chapman replied:

> Well, I converted to the Lord at sixteen, before the shooting. I know a lot of people have a hard time understanding that—how could someone who is quote-unquote born again shoot someone. And my answer to that is, after thinking about it deeply: If you were God, you wouldn't want a bunch of robots running around. He gives us free will. We are free agents. We can do what we want. He specifically told me—I don't want to sound like one of those preachers on TV, but He told my heart, let's put it that way—He told my heart and He let me know, don't kill. I don't want you to kill. He doesn't like murder; the first baby born was a murderer. But I chose to kill someone. I went against what He wanted me to do.[6]

After his "conversion," Chapman became involved in sexual sin, harbored hatred and bitterness, fed his mind on filthy literature, and prayed to Satan, and yet, after the cowardly, cold-blooded shooting of another human being, he still claimed that he was a Christian. This interview reveals how shallow his roots really were. He had no idea of what it means to be a genuine, biblical "Christian." And he wasn't the first. Judas, by some folks' estimation, could have been termed a "Christian." And yet, Jesus, knowing that Judas planned to betray Him, never referred to him as a godly man who just happened to fall into sin. Referring specifically to His betrayer, He said, "One of you is a devil" (John 6:70).

A genuine convert lives only for the will of God. Everything he does is in respect to God's smile or frown. At conversion he prays, "Not my will, but Yours be done," and that's the law by which he lives. He doesn't harbor hatred or bitterness—he knows that if he doesn't forgive, he will not be forgiven. Neither does he cold-bloodedly plan to kill someone, then shoot him in the back. We are told to love our enemies, and to do good to those who despitefully use us. (See Matthew 5:44.) A Christian knows that if he doesn't have love, his faith is worth nothing (1 Corinthians 13). If Mark Chapman had been a Christian, he would have prayed for John Lennon, and when he had the opportunity, he would have shared the gospel with him. Instead, he used the wicked and cowardly murder of another man as a stepping-stone for his own twisted ego.

Look at the difference between those who have the Spirit of God within and those who don't:

But the fruit of the Spirit is love, joy, peace, longsuffering, kindness, goodness, faithfulness, gentleness, self-control. Against such there is no law. And those who are Christ's have crucified the flesh with its passions and desires. . . . [But] the works of the flesh . . . are: adultery, fornication, uncleanness, lewdness, idolatry, sorcery, hatred, contentions, jealousies, outbursts of wrath, selfish ambitions, dissensions, heresies, envy, murders, drunkenness, revelries, and the like; of which I tell you beforehand, just as I also told you in time past, that those who practice such things will not inherit the kingdom of God. (Galatians 5:22–24, 20–21)

Look at what Jesus said about love: "You have heard that it was said, *'You shall love your neighbor* and hate your enemy.' But I say to you, love your enemies, bless those who curse you, do good to those who hate you, and pray for those who spitefully use you and persecute you, that you may be sons of your Father in heaven; for He makes His sun rise on the evil and on the good, and sends rain on the just and on the unjust" (Matthew 5:43–45; emphasis added). He also said, "And as ye would that men should do to you, do ye also to them likewise" (Luke 6:31 KJV).

Jesus said that by men's fruits, you shall know them (Matthew 7:16). "And even now the ax is laid to the root of the trees," he said in the same chapter.

"Therefore every tree which does not bear good fruit is cut down and thrown into the fire" (Matthew 3:10).

But even the right fruit means nothing if it doesn't come from a heart of love. The apostle Paul wrote, "And though I bestow all my goods to feed the poor, and though I give my body to be burned, and have not charity, it profits me nothing" (1 Corinthians 13:3 KJV).

And John the apostle neatly summed it up: "He that loves not knows not God; for God is love" (1 John 4:8).

So to be biblical, instead of painting Chapman as a Christian who fell into sin, he should be seen as a demon-serving, cold, hate-filled, *calculating* Judas. Here's proof.

On Monday, December 8, 1980, around mid-morning, he awakened in his hotel room at the Sheraton—and decided that this was the day he would kill John Lennon:

> He took out the hotel Bible, opened it to the beginning of "The Gospel of John" and wrote in the word "Lennon" after "John." . . .
>
> On his way to the Dakota, he made a stop to buy the copy of *The Catcher in the Rye* he had forgotten the previous night. . . .

Paul Goresh, an amateur photographer who often staked out the Lennons and whom Chapman had seen there on Saturday, joined him. Then Jude Stein appeared again. She told him that she and her friend Jerry had held a conversation with Lennon on Saturday after Chapman left.

Chapman offered to buy her lunch. Afterwards, they returned to the Dakota. Five-year-old Sean Lennon came out with his nanny. Jude introduced Chapman to him and Chapman shook hands with the boy.

Chapman would tell Gaines: "He was the cutest little boy I ever saw. It didn't enter my mind that I was going to kill this poor young boy's father and he won't have a father for the rest of his life. I mean, I love children. I'm the Catcher in the Rye."[7]

Looking back years later, he said, "I had to usurp someone else's importance, someone else's success . . . I was Mr. Nobody until I killed the biggest somebody on Earth."[8]

In 2010, he confessed that he chose to kill Lennon outside the Dakota building because it "wasn't quite as cloistered" as places where other stars on his list could be found. It was then that it was discovered that his hit list included Johnny Carson, the famous American talk show host, and actress Elizabeth

Taylor, among others. However, Lennon seemed to be the easiest target. Chapman told the parole board: "He seemed more accessible to me." Again, Chapman reaffirmed his motive: "It wasn't about them, necessarily, it was just about me. It was all about me at the time." He added: "If it wasn't Lennon, it could have been someone else."[9] This dashes the speculation some had that Lennon had been murdered because of his, "We are more popular than Jesus" remark, made years earlier.

According to the transcript, Chapman said he targeted Lennon, Carson, and Taylor "because they were famous, that was it." He thought that by killing them, John in particular, he would cause the world to notice him: "I felt that by killing John Lennon I would become somebody[,] and instead of that I became a murderer[,] and murderers are not somebodies."[10]

In the past, he had said that he also considered killing Paul McCartney and President Ronald Reagan.[11]

The difference between the true and the false convert is that the Christian *falls* (against his will) into sin, while the hypocrite *dives* (willingly) into sin. Though the one who falls into sin still makes the ultimate decision whether or not to sin, his sin is not a premeditated act. In contrast, if I get up on a

Monday morning and say to myself, "Today I plan to sin," then I need to seriously examine myself and see if I am truly converted. Chapman *planned* murder. He allowed hatred to fester in his soul. He wallowed in self-pity. He fed his mind with blasphemy and sexual sin. He was a devious, callous, jealous, bitter, conniving murderer who shot a man who had just shown him kindness. And then he calmly read his favorite book. He was a hypocrite of the worst kind. Mark David Chapman's "I converted to the Lord at sixteen," truly demonstrates a shallow understanding of the Christian faith.

John had many sins. He was adulterous, blasphemous, and foulmouthed, but to his credit, he admitted the weaknesses in his character, and in view of contemporary "Christianity," I can certainly understand his perspective when it comes to religious hypocrisy. But it was a mistake for him to lay the problems of the world at the doorstep of Christianity.

His 1971 song "Imagine"[12] begins with John dreaming of a world where there is no religious infighting, because people are living for today rather than for eternity. The famous words tell us to imagine that there's no heaven, and that there's no hell below us.

Next the song imagines world peace, with no

borders and wars—wars often sparked by religion, as in the case of Islam, whose agenda is to conquer the world through violent means. John Lennon wanted humanity to give peace a chance. He was sincere, and he wasn't "the only one." An entire generation was tired of war. If only peace and love could have their way, he believed, then the world would "be as one."

Then "Imagine" truly needed the human imagination. John asked the world to imagine having no belongings (as we have seen, he was criticized for having such a dream when he was worth hundreds of millions of dollars, and rode around in limos). He asked his hearers to "imagine no possessions."

But his words were truly just an imagination. Humanity can never have peace with one another until we find peace with God. We can imagine that there's no heaven or hell—it is easy if you try—but it's not reality. Heaven exists as a real place, and so does hell. So whatever we may imagine, we mustn't live in the dreamworld of our imagination. That's a delusion. Don't live just for today. If you do, God Himself calls you a "fool."[13]

In the next chapter, we will begin to look at the fascinating spirituality of the other three Beatles.

THE TALE OF SIR PAUL

When you first get money, you buy all these things
so no one thinks you're mean, and you spread it
around. You get a chauffeur and you find yourself
thrown around the back of this car and you think,
I was happier when I had my own little car! I could
drive myself![1]

~ *Paul McCartney*

JAMES PAUL MCCARTNEY was born
in Liverpool on June 18, 1942. His mother,
Mary, worked as a nurse and midwife at
the Liverpool General Hospital, where he was born.
Jim, his father, was a salesman and led the Jim

Mac's Jazz Band, playing the piano. Paul grew up studying arts and music, including classical piano and guitar, and when he was eleven, he passed the scholarship exam in Liverpool, gaining a place at the Liverpool Institute for Boys. He studied there from 1953 until 1960 and achieved A's in English and Art. During this time, he also sang, composed, and played the bass, acoustic, and electric guitars; piano and keyboards; and, amazingly, more than forty other musical instruments.

His beloved mother died from breast cancer when he was only fourteen, and it was then that he wrote his first song. As mentioned earlier, shortly thereafter he met John Lennon at a local church festival, after which, he joined John's band, the Quarrymen. Later, with George Harrison and Pete Best, the band became the Beatles.

Many of the more popular Beatles' songs were composed by Paul McCartney. Among them were "Yesterday," "Let It Be," "All My Loving," "Eleanor Rigby," "Blackbird," "Hello Goodbye," "Lady Madonna," "Hey Jude," "Long and Winding Road," "Yellow Submarine," "When I'm 64," and "Sgt. Pepper's Lonely Hearts Club Band." Nonetheless, John and Paul established an oral agreement when they were still teenagers, saying that all songs would be credited to both their names, regardless of who really wrote them. That gave them fifty-fifty credit for more than 240 of the songs the Beatles created.[2]

In 1963, the Beatles were interviewed by Jane Asher, after which the BBC photographer asked them to pose with her. That was the beginning of a five-year relationship between Jane and Paul. She became the inspiration for love songs such as "All My Loving," "And I Love Her," "I'm Looking Through You," "You Won't See Me," "We Can Work It Out," "Here, There and Everywhere," and "For No One." The couple announced their engagement on Christmas Day of 1967. However, Asher ended the engagement early in 1968, after discovering Paul in bed with another woman.[3] They attempted to mend the relationship, but it ended permanently and publicly when, on July 20, 1968, Asher announced to the BBC that they were no longer engaged.

Paul's wife of nearly thirty years was American photographer Linda Eastman, who had photographed the Doors, the Who, Jimi Hendrix, Bob Dylan, Otis Redding, Simon and Garfunkel, and the Beach Boys. In 1965, during the filming of *Help!*, she photographed the Beatles—although she didn't meet any of them until 1967 when they were in London. During that time, she was introduced to Paul. They met again when he was in New York for a press conference, at which time she gave him her phone number, and some days later, he contacted her.

A month later, they met and spent a week together, and their relationship developed. Linda recalled, "I came over and we lived together for a while, neither of us talked about marriage, we just loved each other and lived together. We liked each other a lot, so being conventional people, one day I thought: okay, let's get married, we love each other, let's make it definite."[4] They were eventually married on March 12, 1969.

After Brian Epstein died in 1967, each of the members' creativity evolved, and after the Beatles broke up, Paul formed his own band called Wings. Wings became one of the most commercial groups in the '70's. "Band on the Run" won two Grammy awards, and "Mull of Kintyre" remained in the number one position for nine weeks in the UK. It kept the position of highest selling single for seven years. "Rockestra" won a Grammy in 1978. The following year, Paul organized "Concerts for the People of Kampuchea," together with Elvis Costello. "Wonderful Christmastime" was released in 1979 and has remained popular ever since.

Paul was arrested in Tokyo in 1980 for marijuana possession and stayed in prison for ten days. The arrest, together with John's murder in December the same year, pushed Paul into seclusion. He was justifiably nervous about being "the next" to be murdered.

He returned to the music world in 1982 with the album *Tug of War*. It was welcomed by the public and received good reviews. He then pursued his career with success, collaborating with both his wife and with Elvis Costello. The '80s saw Paul's hit "No More Lonely Nights" and his first compilation titled, *All the Best*. He decided to start touring for the first time since John's murder in 1989.

Paul and the remaining Beatles got together in 1994 to produce *The Beatles Anthology* TV documentary series, which was watched by 420 million people in 1995. They recorded and arranged their voices and instruments to a tape kept by Yoko Ono of a song titled "Free as a Bird," written by John in 1977. It was mixed and recorded in the Abbey Road Studios by George Martin.

During the 1990s, Paul focused on composing classical works for the Royal Liverpool Philharmonic Society. In 1995, he released the album *Flaming Pie*. Sad to say, around the same time, his wife was diagnosed with breast cancer. On a happier note, though, that same year,[5] Queen Elizabeth II knighted him as Sir Paul McCartney for his services to music.[6]

In April 1998, Linda, his wife of almost thirty years and mother of their four children, tragically died of breast cancer. After her death, Paul suffered a deep depression and had to receive medical treatment. He remained away from the public eye most of the time for the rest of the year.

He went back to the studio in 1999 and produced an album called *Run Devil Run*. He also released a classical album, *Working Classical*, in November 1999. *A Garland for Linda*, released in 2000, was a choral tribute album that raised funds for cancer survivors.

In 2000, Paul began a romantic relationship with disabled ex-model Heather Mills. They became engaged in 2001. Unfortunately, the same year, on September 11, Paul was seated on a plane in New York when he saw the World Trade Center tragedy before his very eyes. Adding to his sadness, his friend and former bandmate George Harrison died of cancer in November.

In 2002, Paul received the Academy Award nomination for his movie song "Vanilla Sky." Then, in June of 2002, Paul married Heather in a castle in Ireland. Beatrice Milly McCartney, their daughter, was born in October 2003. (However, four years later, Paul and Heather were divorced.)

Also, in 2003, Paul's show "Back in the U.S.S.R." in Moscow's Red Square was attended by former opponents from the KBG; President Vladimir Putin was also present. Paul was a guest of honor in the Kremlin, and in 2004, he received a birthday gift from the Russian president.

In 2006, Paul's first guitar—the one with which he had so impressed John so many years before—was auctioned for more than six hundred thousand dollars.

Paul left EMI in 2007, after forty-five years and signed with Hear Music, a Los Angeles company. He then released the album *Memory Almost Full*, which included mandolin sounds. In June, he appeared together with Ringo Starr, Olivia Harrison, and Yoko Ono in a live broadcast with Gui Laliberte (Cirque du Soleil) from the Revolution Lounge at the Mirage hotel and casino in Las Vegas.

That same year, Paul released a three-DVD set called *The McCartney Years* which contains more than forty music videos and live performances. His choral album *Ecco Cor Meum (Behold My Heart)* was voted the Classical Album of the year.

Sir Paul McCartney is considered one of the most successful entertainers ever. He has played a huge role in shaping our culture, being a composer, lead singer, author, poet, artist, humanitarian, and entrepreneur. He is listed in the *Guinness Book of World Records* as the "'most successful musician and composer in popular music history,'" with sixty gold discs to his credit, and "sales of 100 million singles in the UK alone."[7] Further, his song "Yesterday" has been covered more than any other song in history.[8] On top of all that, he played the largest public solo performance, with 350,000-plus people in attendance, in Brazil in 1989.[9] He also holds more than three thousand copyrights.

· 12 ·

PAUL McCARTNEY AND GOD

I'm not religious, but I'm very spiritual.[1]

~ *Paul McCartney*

PAUL WAS BAPTIZED a Roman Catholic but was raised nondenominationally. His father, James McCartney, was a Protestant who professed to be an agnostic.[2] Mary, his mother, was Roman Catholic. That may be the reason many have wrongly surmised that "Let it Be" was about Paul's Catholic faith. That impression is understandable when you listen to the words. He said that when he found himself in times of trouble "Mother Mary comes to me." She told him to "Let it be, let it be," whispering words of wisdom, to let it be.[3]

However, the inspiration for the song came from a dream he had while he was recording the *White Album.*" In the dream, he saw his beloved mother, Mary, who had died of cancer in 1956, when Paul was only fourteen, telling him, "It will be all right; just let it be." It was his mother, not the Virgin Mary, to whom he was referring when he wrote the "Mother Mary" lyric. Paul said, "It was great to visit with her again. I felt very blessed to have that dream. So that got me writing 'Let It Be.'"[4]

Paul's mother was a health visitor and midwife who rode her bicycle to visit patients. After she was diagnosed with cancer, she bravely continued to ride her bike even though, at times, she had trouble breathing (she was a heavy smoker) and had increasing pain. The last words she spoke were to Dill Mohan, her sister-in-law. She said, "I would love to have seen the boys growing up."

Paul named his daughter, Mary, after his beloved mother. His younger brother, Michael, said that their father courageously carried on and was there for them after their mother died. "We both owe him a lot. He stayed home and looked after us."[5]

As detailed earlier, each of the Beatles at the height of Beatlemania was an apparent atheist. "Religion," said Paul, back in 1963, was something he didn't think about: "It doesn't fit in with my life."[6] While touring Britain in October 1964, he told *Playboy*, "None of us believe in God," though John quickly clarified the group's position as "more agnostic than atheistic."[7]

Time mellowed Paul's atheism. In an interview published in *Reader's Digest* in 2001, he spoke of the miracles of inspiration and childbirth, saying:

> I don't understand it at all. But I love it. I think life is quite mysterious and quite miraculous. I mean, when I saw my first baby, Mary, born, I remember just thinking, "That is magic." I know how we did it. But there's still a miracle happening. I still don't know how I write songs. And I don't want to know. Every time I come to write a song there's this sort of magic little thing where I go, "Ooh, ooh, it's happening again. Ooh, ooh, ooh." I'm just thrilling myself with this sort of thing. And I do it all the time. I just sort of sit down at the piano and go, "Oh, my God. I don't know this one." And suddenly there's like a song there.[8]

I can identify with Paul. Before my conversion, I wept at the birth of my first child. I was thinking, *This is a miracle*, and saying, "Thank you, thank you . . ." but amazingly, I never thought that God had anything to do with it.

Where do ideas and thoughts and inspiration for music come from? They do seem to magically appear. It's illogical, but so much in life defies logic, and without reference to God, it has no explanation. If a Creator doesn't exist, we are simply a species of animal who finds ourselves on a huge hunk of dirt, spinning through space, not knowing where we came from or where we are heading. We not only take life and our existence for granted; we even take for granted everyday life, in which there are many things that are illogical.

Flight isn't logical. How can incredibly heavy planes filled with people float across the sky? Logic says that everything heavy falls. Without knowledge of the invisible law of aerodynamics, flight seems miraculous. Neither is the phenomenon of television logical. I regularly sit in California and watch *live* football the very second it happens, seven thousand miles away in New Zealand. All this is done through a box with a glass front. It doesn't make sense. How can I watch video on my wireless iPod, and send e-mail messages from it to people on the other side of the world? If there were wires involved, I could probably grasp it, but all this video-sending happens invisibly. I can send music, video, letters, books, and 101 things, all on a device that sits in the palm of my hand. It's illogical and arguably fits the category of "miraculous."

In the same interview, Paul spoke of the type of faith he has:

> This is life. We're born, we die. But, with creativity, I just have a faith. It's not a faith of any particular religion because I worry that religions start wars. It's a great spiritual belief that there is something really great there that I probably refer to as a spirit of goodness. I'm doing a choral piece at the moment for a choir in Oxford. I sort of talk to a spirit of goodness, because I don't want to alienate Catholics, Jewish people, Muslims. 'Cause I know we're all good, there's good in all of us. But that's my belief, that there is something sort of magical there. And that was what helped me write "Yesterday." I don't quite know what it is. Something to do with me, something to do with my love of music and my faith in the process. But I don't quite know what it is and I don't want to know.[9]

Paul's "I worry that religions start wars" is reasonable. Religion comes in as number two for causing historical atrocities. Number one is atheistic communism, which has taken the lives of more than 100 million people. But the problem runs deeper than either "religion" or "atheism." Wars are caused by *people.* Human beings fight and kill over land, politics, money, women, and a million other things. So it seems strange to speak of the atrocities of religion, and in the next breath say, "I know that we are all good." However, in view of the prevailing culture, I can still understand why he would say such a thing.

In 2010, a private Christian school in Dallas, Texas, refused to enroll a child because the child's parents were lesbians. In a statement, school authorities said, "We regret the disappointment the mother feels, but also do not understand why she would want to enroll her child in a school that would undercut her own personal values at home." Surprisingly, the child's mother agreed with the school, saying, "I absolutely would not want her to partake in a school where they did not believe or condone the relationship that we have together." The school had previously rejected an applicant who came from a homosexual household, fired an unmarried teacher who became pregnant, and removed a man "from leadership roles in the school" after he left his wife for another woman. The lesbian mother said she was raised in a Baptist home, so she felt the school could give her child a good education and impart "the basic Bible teachings . . . follow the Golden Rule, the Ten Commandments, be kind to your neighbor." But she added, "The God that I know and the God that I love will love me and love my children no matter what."[10]

When human beings don't like God's moral standards, it's very common for us to make up our own god. But in doing so, we violate the second of the Ten Commandments: "You shall not make yourself a graven image..." This was Israel's problem right down through their history. They strayed from God's law into idolatry, then into sexual sin, and then into judgment. God never changes, even if we imagine Him to be something other than He is. He is deeply offended by homosexuality, and He's not just "a spirit of goodness."

If God is an unintelligent spirit of goodness, then humanity doesn't have a problem. But if He is intelligent and therefore cares about morality, we are all in big trouble. In the light of creation, our intuitive morality, and desire for justice, we cannot believe that God is an ignorant entity. If you think otherwise, try making a frog, a leaf, a flower, or a bird, *from nothing*. The Creator is clearly unspeakably intelligent, and if He is also good and therefore moral, He *must* see that ultimate justice is done. He cannot let a man murder and rape without bringing him to justice.

But Paul's belief in God does go a little deeper than his "spirit of goodness." After John was violently murdered and George was stabbed in the chest, we know that Paul became concerned for his own safety. Any crazy person (even *one* of the millions of fans) could see himself becoming renowned by killing a Beatle. After all, George was almost murdered. In 1984, the *New York Times* said that he confessed, "After what happened to John, I'm absolutely terrified."[11] He had reason to be worried: "In 1990, George was sent a series of death threats at home, and two years later, the police found an obsessed Beatles fan lurking around his house, apparently with the intention of burning it down."[12]

So it was in the light of these fears that Paul began to talk about "the Man upstairs," saying that it was God who would determine when his number was up. The interview revealed that he not only believed in God, but that he also believed in some sort of afterlife. This is what he said in 2001:

> **King**: Where do you live?
>
> **McCartney**: I live in England, two hours south of London.
>
> **King**: Do you have high security?
>
> **McCartney**: Yes.

King: Based on what happened to John.

McCartney: Yes.

King: What happened to George.

McCartney: Yes.

King: You must worry?

McCartney: Yes. Well, I don't worry, you know, because . . .

King: You don't.

McCartney: No, because the moment the Man upstairs wants me, I'm his. You know, it's . . .

King: You believe that?

McCartney: Yes. I know that.

King: You know that.

McCartney: Well, I know that at some point I'm going to die, and that's it, so I don't worry about it.

King: But you do have security. I mean . . .

McCartney: I try and avoid it, by the way.

(LAUGHTER)[13]

Linda died at the age of fifty-six on April 17, 1998, in Tucson, Arizona, at the McCartney ranch. She had earlier confided, "My mother was killed in a plane crash, so I hate traveling in planes. Death is so unexpected. I would actually rather stay at home and not go anywhere."[14] Back in 1962, just before 10 a.m., American Airlines flight number 1 left New York, heading for Los Angeles. At 1,500 feet, it plunged into Jamaica Bay, and exploded on contact 50 feet from the shore, tragically killing all ninety-five people on board, including her fifty-five-year-old Jewish mom, Louise Eastman, mother of four children.

In 1992, Linda spoke briefly about her Jewish background:

> **DF**: Do you feel totally removed from your one-half Jewishness now?
>
> **Linda**: I'm all Jewish.
>
> **DF**: Your mother was Jewish? I thought your mother was a WASP.[15]
>
> **Linda**: No, my parents were both Jews. I think my mother's people were Alsatian.
>
> **DF**: I can't believe that all these years I've been imagining your mother as this horsey, WASPy type.
>
> **Linda**: She was WASPy, but she was Jewish. You know, Danny, you're much more into all this than I am. I could never get into all that stuff, I'm very not into religion.
>
> **DF**: Did your parents observe any Jewish holidays or anything like that?
>
> **Linda**: I think they tried to have something for Passover once, and we all made fun of it, and we all hated it. I've always hated religion. It's the most guilt-ridden, horrible thing. "My God is better than yours, and I'm going to fight you and

kill you because of your religion." I think it's just
a sick idea. You know how people are colour-blind
when it comes to other people—I mean, hopefully
they are. Well, I'm religious-blind.[16]

In April 1999, when Arthur, Paul's first grand-
child, was born, Paul said to a number of friends,
"He's a very clever little lad. His mother is Jewish and
his father is Christian, so he chose to be born between
Passover and Easter."[17]

Linda's tragic death seemed to deepen his spirituality:

> Mary, Paul and Linda's daughter and the
> mother of little Arthur, is of course one-half
> Jewish. Paul . . . says, "His mother is Jewish."
> We now have Paul being more upfront about
> Linda's religion than Linda ever was. No one had
> ever heard him describe his children as "Jewish"
> before—Chrissie Hynde thinks that now that
> Linda is gone, Paul is cherishing everything
> about her even more than he did during all their
> years together. Including her religion of birth,
> which she cared about not at all.[18]

When CNN's Larry King asked Paul, "Do you
think Linda is somewhere?" he answered, "Yes, she's
here. Sort of. In a kind of dimensional thing. I don't
know. I don't—I don't have any sort of very strong

religious beliefs. But I have kind of—I have spiritual feelings about that kind of thing."[19]

All this came on the heels of the famous rumors that he was already dead. It must have been a little unnerving for the whole world to think that you are dead and buried.

PAUL IS DEAD

The "Paul is dead" hoax is considered by some to be the most elaborate pop deception in history. In 1969, shortly after the release of the *Abbey Road* album, a DJ in Detroit, Michigan, known as Russ Gibb, received a call from a student at Eastern Michigan University. The caller, Tom, said live on the air that the song "Revolution 9" had a hidden message when played backwards; a voice says, "Turn me on, dead man." He also said that in the end of "Strawberry Fields Forever," a deep voice says, "I buried Paul." The DJ played both songs on the air, and the phones in the station wouldn't stop ringing.

Since then, Beatles fans have found what they believe are hundreds of clues hidden in their album covers and lyrics. All clues point to a car accident Paul had back in 1966, when, the myth says, he died and was replaced by William Campbell, who was a winner in a Paul look-alike contest. They believe that with a little training and surgery, he took Paul's place.

Perhaps the most popular clue is *Abbey Road*'s album cover, where Paul appears walking barefooted; John is leading; all dressed in white; Ringo is in a suit; and in the back is George, in jeans. This, fans say, represents a funeral procession where John is the religious figure; Ringo, a grieving family member; Paul, the dead person; and George, the gravedigger.

The rumor was so big that it was covered by *Time* magazine and the *New York Times*. *Life* magazine sent a group of reporters to Paul's farm in Scotland to find out the truth, and did a cover story. Paul agreed to a photo session with his family and appeared in the story, titled "Paul Is Still with Us," for the November 7, 1969, issue.

A short time after the 2001 Larry King interview, Paul found himself confronted with the reality of death once again. In a statement after the terrible passing of fifty-eight-year-old George, who succumbed to the ravages of lung cancer, Paul, then sixty-six, said, "We held hands. It's funny, even at the height of our friendship, as guys, you'd never hold hands." He added, "I sat with him for a few hours when he was in treatment about ten days from his death. We joked about things—just amusing, nutty stuff. It was good. It was like we were dreaming."[20]

The two of them met on a bus when they were schoolboys in Liverpool. Paul said that George was like family to him. "He was my little baby brother, almost, because I'd known him that long."[21] He also said, "Something like George passing, it makes you think, 'God, things are so impermanent: suddenly there's this little friend of mine, he used to get on the bus, and now he's passed away.' There's that whole lifetime of a friendship that physically has ended, not emotionally."[22]

One writer said, "McCartney has also made peace with his mortality, having survived the premature deaths of John Lennon, George Harrison, and the love of his life, Linda. On the 'End of the End,' the last tune in the five-song suite, he looks death in the eye and smiles:

On the day that I die
I'd like jokes to be told
And stories of old
To be rolled out like carpets
That children have played on
And laid on while listening
To stories of old.[23]

But the only ones who can look death in the eye and smile are those who have escaped its cold grip. Otherwise we are like prisoners on death row, awaiting execution. Paul said:

> I'm kind of fatalistic about it really. I know when John died, people sort of said, "Are you really worried?" I said, "No." When your number's up, it's up. I concentrate on living day to day. I don't know what I'd like my funeral to be outside of the track on the album ["End of the End"] and I'm not even sure if I want *that*. It'd be kind of good for people to . . . celebrate your life rather than sit around moaning. It's something I don't really think about too much. I'm too busy living. I just enjoy what I do and get on with it.[24]

When Paul says he doesn't think much about his death, I can't help but doubt him. We all think about it, especially as time passes and it gets closer by the minute. Without the Savior, we are stuck with fatalism, pessimism, and futility. There is no consolation in death if we are godless. In my twenty-two years of godlessness, I didn't give too much thought to the existence of God. I just wanted to get on with living. But I couldn't escape the reality that time was like the ever-passing sand in an hourglass.

Death is simply the result of our sin. We can't

separate the crime from the punishment. Sin has wages, just as in many countries, murder has a death sentence. Unpleasant though the subject may be, it's good to think about death because it's the first sign of being awakened to doing something about it. Don't resign yourself to death's inevitability. The same God who created you in the womb offers you the gift of everlasting life, and until you are born again, you will have as much understanding of that new life as you did when you were surrounded by water in the darkness of your preborn state. At that point of your existence, you couldn't begin to conceive of what was in store for you. You were going to be birthed into a world of light, color, air, love, language, sound, laughter, birds, sky, sunshine, and love. There is one thing you need for that to become a reality. You must have the oxygen of understanding. Without the knowledge of sin, you will never see light. So don't be afraid of the Law of God. Let the Ten Commandments show you that you need the Savior. Then repent and trust in Jesus, and you will see the light and become a new person on the inside. You will be born again.

THE BEACH BOYS

We tend to use the English language without too much thought. Take, for example, the short phrase "God only knows." It rolls off the tongue of the ungodly without too much thought, other than to express something that is inexpressible. However, its implications are more than huge. God is omniscient. He knows *everything*. He knows every thought of every one of the six billion–plus people that inhabit this earth. Think of how many thoughts pass through your own head in an hour. There are probably thousands, and each thought lines up for its turn as though there is no tomorrow.

We hardly give a thought to the fact that we think continually, twenty-four hours a day, eight days a week.[25] It never stops. Even while we sleep, we think. Now think of the trillions of thoughts that pass through the minds of the hundreds of billions of people who have lived for the thousands of years that humanity has existed, in the hundreds of complex languages in which people think; then mumble to yourself, "*God only knows* what they thought.*" The thought is so profound, it is beyond human comprehension.

In 1966, the Beach Boys released a complex song called "God Only Knows" on the group's eleventh studio album, *Pet Sounds*. It was composed by the genius of the band, Brian Wilson, and broke new ground in that it was the first commercial pop song to have the name of God in its title. That was radical in the godless world. It was a song Paul loved, and in a 1990 interview, he said:

> It's a really, really great song—it's a big favorite of mine. I was asked recently to give my top ten favorite songs for a Japanese radio station . . . I didn't think long and hard on it but I popped that ["God Only Knows"] on the top of my list. It's very deep. Very emotional, always a bit of a choker for me, that one. There are certain songs that just hit home with me, and they're the strangest collection of songs . . . but that is high on the list, I must say . . . "God Only Knows" lyrics are great. Those do it to me every time.[26]

Speaking on a special Radio 1 show to mark the British station's fortieth anniversary, Paul also said, "'God Only Knows' is one of the few songs that reduces me to tears every time I hear it. It's really just a love song, but it's brilliantly done. It shows the genius of Brian . . . I've actually performed it with him and I'm afraid to say that during the sound check I broke down. It was just too much to stand there singing this song that does my head in and to stand there singing it with Brian."[27]

For more than two decades, I "believed" in God. For many of those years, I prayed each night. But I was blind to the reality of God. I believed that Jesus died on the cross, but if you had questioned me as to why He died, I couldn't have told you, other than to say that He was murdered by those who hated Him. I didn't understand that He was God in human form, taking the sin of the world upon Himself, so that humanity could have everlasting life. Paul revealed an intellectual understanding of who Jesus was, when he said, "John's time and effort were, in the main, spent on pretty honorable stuff. As for the other side, well, nobody's perfect, nobody's Jesus. And look what they did to him."[28]

His words reveal a knowledge that Jesus was a perfect human being, or close to it. But they also reveal that he (like me) had no real understanding of what happened two thousand years ago, and that everlasting life is only as far away as repentance and faith in the Savior.

What about your understanding? Do you realize that God has a specially wrapped gift of eternal life *just for you*? If so, then what's stopping you from coming to Jesus Christ *right now* and receiving God's gift of everlasting life?

· 13 ·

GEORGE'S
STORY

We made our money and fame, but for me that
wasn't it . . . It was good fun for a while, but it
certainly wasn't the answer to what life is about.[1]

~ *George Harrison*

GEORGE HARRISON[2] was born on February 25, 1943, in Liverpool, England. His mother, Louise, worked in a store, and his father, Harold, as a steward on a ship. George and his three siblings were raised as Roman Catholics.

When he was fourteen, George would sit in the back of his classroom, drawing guitars in his school-books, at the Liverpool Institute for Boys. Soon he formed a skiffle group named Rebels with his brother, Peter, and a close friend.

George joined the Quarrymen after Paul McCartney talked to John Lennon about him. John thought George was too young, but he was accepted into the band nevertheless. In 1960, the band was offered a job in Hamburg. However, their first trip to Hamburg was short-lived, as George was deported for being underage.

George became the lead guitar player with the Beatles, and after Brian Epstein became their manager in 1961, the group rocketed to success by 1963.

By 1965, the four Beatles were appointed Members of the Order of the British Empire. Harrison's guitar playing represents the style of the '60s and served as a model for many other musicians. In 1966, his relationship and involvement with the group reached its peak with the album *Revolver* and his collaboration on three songs and new ideas influenced by Indian music and the sitar.[3]

George met model Pattie Boyd in 1966 while filming the movie *A Hard Day's Night*. They were married that same year.

While filming the movie *Help!* in the Bahamas, a Hindu devotee gave a book about reincarnation to each of the band members. George then spent some time in India with his wife and visited several gurus and Indian holy places. In 1968, he traveled with the rest of the band to India to study meditation with the Maharishi Mahesh Yogi.

Tensions within the group caused George to quit the Beatles for twelve days in early 1969, but after negotiations at two business meetings, he returned to the band. That summer, he produced the single "Hare Krishna Mantra" which was performed by devotees in London's Radha Krishna Temple. Later in the year, he met A. C. Bhaktivedanta Swami Prabhupda, founder of the International Society for Krishna Consciousness, and, soon after, George embraced the Hare Krishna tradition for life, especially *japa-yoga*, which is meditative chanting, using a string of beads to count the repetitions.

George's relationship with the other Beatles was very close. Paul often referred to him as his "baby brother."[4] John said, "[George] was like a disciple of mine when we started."[5] But after George published his autobiography, *I Me Mine*, John was hurt and upset because he was mentioned only in passing. Toward the end of John's life, their relationship was not good. However, George paid him tribute after he was murdered, with the song "All Those Years Ago."

By 1970, before the Beatles split up, George had already released two solo albums: *Wonderwall Music* and *Electronic Sound*, both instrumental. The last years of the Beatles were hard for George, because the rest of the group didn't want to record many of his songs. By the time the group dissolved, he still had a great deal of unreleased material. His first real solo album was released after the breakup, and was named *All Things Must Pass*. It was a triple album, containing many of the songs George had already written but hadn't been able to record with the Beatles. It was a commercial success and it is regarded as his best album, including other musicians, such as Eric Clapton, Dave Mason, Billy Preston, and Ringo Starr.

George was sued for copyright infringement over his number-one hit song "My Sweet Lord," as it was markedly similar to the Chiffons song "He's so Fine," released in 1963 and owned by Bright Tunes. In 1981, a judge in the case decided that George had "subconsciously" plagiarized the song, and he was ordered to pay $1,599,987 to Bright Tunes. Then, George's manager, Allen Klein, bought Bright Tunes and continued the suit. The judge ruled that Klein had acted improperly and that George would have to pay $587,000 to Klein, the amount Klein had paid for Bright Tunes. Klein didn't win anything from the deal, and George became the owner of the rights of both "My Sweet Lord" and "He's So Fine." This ended the plagiarism claim, though the dispute lasted until into the 1990s.

In 1971, George organized the Concert for Bangladesh with Indian musician Ravi Shankar, to raise money for refugees of the Bangladesh Liberation War. The event, featuring artists such as Badfinger, Eric Clapton, and Bob Dylan, attracted more than forty thousand people to New York's Madison Square Garden.

For the next few years, George continued to write music, produce, and release albums. He also performed in public and appeared on several TV shows.

In 1974, his marriage ended when wife Pattie left him and moved in with Eric Clapton. George remarried in 1978, to secretary Olivia Trinidad Arias, whom he had met at Dark Horse Records. Their son, Dhani, was born that same year.

After the murder of John Lennon in 1980, George began to live in fear for his life. In 1984, he confided, "After what happened to John, I'm absolutely terrified."[6] He had reason to be worried. In 1990, a series of death threats were sent to his home, and two years later, the police found an obsessed Beatles fan lurking around his house, apparently intending to burn it down.

Friar Park, the Harrisons' estate, situated on thirty-four acres and containing dozens of rooms, was in Henley-on-Thames, twenty-five miles west of London. The locals called it Fort Knox because of its many security measures, which included powerful lights, video cameras, a razor-wire fence, and electronically controlled gates.

But in spite of these precautions, at 3:30 in the morning on December 30, 1999, an intruder broke into the estate. The assailant, armed with a seven-inch knife, entered Friar Park, after breaking a window. The attacker hit George's wife, Olivia, on the head and repeatedly stabbed George when he went to his wife's aid. The brave couple fought the assailant, inflicting head injuries and holding him down while staff called the police.

The former Beatle was treated at a nearby hospital for a collapsed lung and various minor stab wounds to his body. Olivia was also treated for cuts and bruises she suffered in the struggle with the intruder.

The assailant was thirty-three-year-old Michael

Abram, a Beatles fan who lived in Liverpool, the hometown of all four Beatles. Abram had nursed an irrational obsession with the Beatles, just as Mark Chapman had with John Lennon. Abram's mother told reporters that her son, a former heroin addict, was mentally ill and that he often heard voices in his head and saw things emerging from walls. She also said that her son hated the Beatles and even believed they were witches.[7]

THE DEATH OF A SECOND BEATLE

In 1997, George was diagnosed with throat cancer, which was attributed to his smoking during the '60s. He was successfully treated with radiotherapy, but in 2001, a cancerous growth had to be removed from one of his lungs. In July, he received radiotherapy in Switzerland, but to no avail.

George Harrison died on November 29, 2001, in his Hollywood Hills mansion. He was cremated and, following Hindu tradition, his ashes were scattered in the Ganges River.

On the first anniversary of Harrison's death, the Concert for George was held at London's Royal Albert Hall. Eric Clapton, Paul McCartney, and Ringo Starr were among those who performed at the event, and the profits were donated to George's charity, the Material World Charitable Foundation.

The Hollywood Chamber of Commerce awarded George a star on the Walk of Fame on April 14, 2009. Son Dhani Harrison uttered the Hare Krishna mantra during the ceremony—a fitting event, attended by actors and musicians, to celebrate the life of a star.

GEORGE HARRISON AND HIS "SWEET LORD"

*I'd never thought about, couldn't even say the word
"God." It embarrassed me, but it was so strange,
God, and it washed away all these fears and doubts
and little things that hang you up.*[1]

~ George Harrison

ALTHOUGH THE BEATLES originally said they didn't believe in God, it wasn't long until that changed, especially for George. His son, Dhani Harrison, said:

You know, I read a letter from him to his mother that he wrote when he was twenty-four. He was on tour or someplace when he wrote it. It basically says, "I want to be self-realized. I want to find God. I'm not interested in material things, this world, fame—I'm going for the real goal. And I hope you don't worry about me, mum." He wrote that when he was twenty-four! And that was basically the philosophy that he had up until the day he died.[2]

As early as 1969, George said that he had begun to understand Jesus and what He taught:

I got to understand what Christ really was through Hinduism. Down through the ages there has always been the spiritual path, it's been passed on, it always will be, and if anybody ever wants it in any age it's always there. It just so happens India was the place where the seed of it was planted. The Himalayas were very inaccessible to people, so they always have peace there. The yogis are the only people who can make it out there. It may be something to do with my past lives, but I felt a great connection with it. In this age the West and East are closer and can all benefit so much from each other. We can help them with our material attributes, and they can help us with their spiritual things.[3]

At a 1974 press conference, George quoted Jesus from the Sermon on the Mount: "Just certain things happened in my life which left me thinking 'What's it all about, Alfie?' and I remembered Jesus said somewhere[,] 'Knock and the door shall be opened' and I said (knock, knock) 'Hellooo!'"[4]

His "What's it all about, Alfie?" is a reference to the 1966 British film *Alfie*, starring Michael Caine. *Alfie* tells the story of a promiscuous young man who, following several life reversals, begins to rethink his purposes and goals in life. In one very moving scene, after Alfie gets a married woman pregnant and encourages her to have an abortion, he arrives after the procedure has taken place and sees the fetus. The film doesn't show the child, but the camera does a close-up of Alfie's face as it contorts and he begins to weep when he realizes that the unborn child is a fully formed little boy. Later on he admits, "I murdered him."[5]

The movie's theme song asks the question of life, "What's it all about, Alfie?" Here are some of the lyrics:

> What's it all about when you sort it out, Alfie?
> What will you lend on an old golden rule?
> As sure as I believe there's a Heaven above, Alfie,
> I know there's something much more,
> Something even non-believers can believe in.[6]

These are the same sorts of questions George Harrison asked: What is life's ultimate purpose? Why do we die? Where is God? Is life simply about pleasure—women, money, sex, fame, music, and then death?

Some unthinking people wait until they are on death's door before they think deeply about the reality of death and life's futility. An atheist once wrote to me, saying:

> What does a trillion years feel like? In light of eternity, even after a trillion years, it's only just "beginning." But it's your choice on where you'll spend eternity. I barely know what to do with myself if I have more than 5 hours of free time. Heaven or Hell . . . BOTH of those seem like torture once the novelty wears off. How do YOU reconcile the inevitable boredom you will feel after having done everything in the Universe two times over in your precious paradise in the clouds? Or is there is [a] "suicide" option in Heaven once you've had enough?

I had to admit to him that I once felt the same way.

I used to think that if I was ever put in prison for my faith, I would pass the time by working out—until one day, when I had to wait for a doctor in a small room that was about the size of a prison cell. The wait turned out to be about thirty minutes. I enthusiastically worked out for the first five, looked at all the horrible posters of lungs and other things on the wall for another five, and then spent the last twenty minutes going crazy with boredom. Some people don't mind doing nothing. Others, like me and perhaps you, need to do something meaningful. However, this sense of boredom drives some to drink, some to drugs, some to suicide, and some to their knees.

The Bible says that when humanity fell because of sin, it brought with it a curse. This Genesis curse subjected the entire human race to futility. No matter what we would put our hands to, it would be transient. Nothing would last. Death would take all. From that moment in time, the curse changed everything. Sure, there was a "high" to be found in the pleasures of this life. But eventually, all became mundane, resulting in boredom. The pleasure in any good experience is only temporary.

But the moment we find peace with God through repentance and faith in Jesus, God seals us with His Holy Spirit and marks us for His coming Kingdom. That's not some harp-playing "spiritual" realm, but life on this earth without the Genesis curse. That means no earthquakes, floods, famines, hurricanes, tornadoes, poisonous snakes, biting tigers, mosquitoes, pain, tears, suffering, cancer, aging, depression, disease, death, dandruff, or dentists. And guess what? No more futility! No more boredom. God promises (and He *cannot* lie), that all those who trust in His mercy will have pleasure "forevermore."

However, instead of looking to the New Testament to find out more about Jesus, George gravitated toward Hinduism. He said:

> The Lord, or God, has got a million names, whatever you want to call him, it doesn't matter as long as you call him, Jesus is on the mainline, tell him what you want. Going back to self-realization, one guru said he found no separation between man and God, saving man's spiritual unadventurousness, and that's the catch, everybody's so unadventurous. We're all conditioned, our consciousness has been so polluted by the material energy it's hard to try and pull it all ways in order to really discover our true nature. Every one of us has within us a drop of that ocean and we have the same qualities as God, just like a drop of the ocean has the same qualities as the whole ocean. Everybody's looking for something and we are it. We don't have to look anywhere—it's right there within ourselves.[7]

So what was this "something" of which George spoke? What was it that liberated us from the pollutions of this world, and how do we access it from "within"? In his song "Awaiting on You All," George tells us what we are to do:

If you open up your heart
You will know what I mean
We've been polluted so long
But here's a way for you to get clean

You don't need no church house
And you don't need no temple
You don't need no rosary beads or them books
to read
To see that you have fallen

By chanting the names of the Lord
and you'll be free
The Lord is awaiting on you all
to awaken and see.[8]

The quiet Beatle believed that chanting the name of the Lord Krishna cleansed one of his sin and pleased God. He once said, "I drove for about twenty-three hours and chanted all the way . . . You know, once you get chanting, then things start to happen transcendentally."[9]

The repetition of certain names and words in religion as a means of getting in God's graces is nothing new. Roman Catholics repeat five "decades" of Hail Marys while praying the rosary. This, and other repetitive practices, has its roots in the history of the Roman Catholic Church:

> Of St. Aybert, in the twelfth century, it is recorded that he recited 150 Hail Marys daily, 100 with genuflections[10] and 50 with prostrations. So Thierry tells us of St. Louis of France that "without counting his other prayers the holy King knelt down every evening fifty times and each time he stood upright then knelt again and repeated slowly an Ave Maria." . . . In this way, owing to the fatigue of these repeated prostrations and genuflections, the recitation of a number of Hail Marys was often regarded as a penitential exercise, and it is recorded of certain canonized saints, e.g. the Dominican nun St. Margaret (d. 1292), daughter of the King of Hungary, that on certain days she recited the Ave a thousand times with a thousand prostrations.[11]

It is believed that repetition earns "divine grace"—in other words, whoever repeats the "Hail Mary" obtains God's favor. The problem is, grace, or divine favor, *cannot* be earned. It can only be freely given by God, and it's not free if we have earned it by doing something. Scripture (from the original Greek language) makes this clear:

> For it is by free grace (God's unmerited favor)
> that you are saved (delivered from judgment and
> made partakers of Christ's salvation) through
> [your] faith. And this [salvation] is not of your-
> selves [of your own doing, it came not through
> your own striving], but it is the gift of God; not
> because of works [not the fulfillment of the Law's
> demands], lest any man should boast. [It is not
> the result of what anyone can possibly do, so no
> one can pride himself in it or take glory to him-
> self.] (Ephesians 2:8–9 AMP)

We are not only in need of grace, but we desperately need God's mercy. Someone explained the
difference between the two this way:

> Suppose I was speeding on the highway and a
> policeman pulls me over. If he doesn't give me
> a ticket, then he gave me mercy. If he gives me
> a $100 bill, then he gave me grace. As sinners,
> we deserve punishment. But, by God's mercy,
> He withholds judgment. Luke 18:13: "And the
> publican, standing afar off, would not lift up so
> much as his eyes unto heaven, but smote upon his
> breast, saying, God be merciful to me a sinner."
> We don't deserve God's goodness, but instead He
> has lavished grace upon us. Ephesians 2:7: "That
> in the ages to come he might show the exceeding
> riches of his grace in his kindness toward us
> through Christ Jesus. For by grace are ye saved
> through faith; and that not of yourselves: it is
> the gift of God" By God's mercy, we escape hell.
> But by God's grace, we receive everlasting life.[12]

In other words, we cannot *earn* God's mercy *or* His grace. Mercy and grace are *always* unmerited. This is the incredibly good news of Christianity. We don't need to chant, pray, do good works, be good, lie on beds of nails, sit on hard pews, go door-to-door, fast, face a certain direction when we pray, or recite Hail Marys to find everlasting life. Eternal life is a free gift of God (Romans 6:23), given to those who repent and *trust* in His Son. That means that anyone can have His favor *without having to strive in any way to earn it.*

God is willing to freely forgive our sins and offer us everlasting life simply because He is rich in mercy, not because we've worked for it. That's the message of the Bible. So why isn't this sinful world getting up from its aching hands and knees and simply receiving this incredible gift that God has to offer?

There's one big reason, and it is made clear in the Scriptures.

According to the New Testament, the Jews thought they could find everlasting life without the help of God: The apostle Paul wrote, "For I bear them witness that they have a zeal for God, but not according to knowledge. For they being ignorant of God's righteousness, and seeking to establish their own righteousness, have not submitted to the righteousness of God. For Christ is the end of the law for righteousness to everyone who believes" (Romans 10:2–4). They had a religious zeal, *but they lacked vital knowledge,* and in their ignorance, they tried to "establish their own righteousness." In other words, they tried to make themselves right, but didn't allow God to make them right with Himself.

Let me try and pass their missing knowledge on to you through a simple analogy. A man burglarized a number of empty houses while the owners were on vacation, and set fire to them as he left to destroy any evidence that he was there. Unbeknownst to him, a homeless man had been asleep in the attic of one of the homes, and had perished in the flames.

The burglar is caught and, clearly responsible for the terrible crime, is found guilty. But to avoid being given life in jail, he decides he will do something to please the judge as he stands before him: he will audibly repeat the judge's name hundreds of times, over and over again.

Such a thought is ludicrous. He's a guilty criminal, so how could he even begin to think that doing such a thing could merit favor in the judge's eyes. The deluded robber *thinks* he can make up for a man's horrifying death by simply reciting the judge's name. In his eyes, that would balance the scales. Such a course can only bring further disdain from the judge for the man's obvious lack of understanding that he was responsible for the death of another human being. To put it another way—*the criminal doesn't see the seriousness of his crime.*

The criminal then takes twenty dollars out of his pocket and tries to hand it to the judge. Instead of that pleasing the court, it will bring further wrath because his effort to give the judge anything isn't seen as a gift, but a despicable attempt to bribe the judge and pervert justice. Can you understand that? This is *so* important.

CLEAN FLIES

I hate flies. They are annoying and so hard to hit unless you have a good flyswatter and a very fast hand. But as much as I hate the fly, I marvel at how incredibly well it is made, from its amazing compound eyes that can see the slightest movement, to its tiny brain that is connected to the eyes and tells the fly to move because it is in danger.

The common housefly is more complex than our most sophisticated airplane. It has a heart that pumps blood through its tiny veins, feet that have the ability to suction its body upside down on a ceiling, and an agility that makes our most maneuverable aircraft look like a fat and slow-moving dinosaur. It has instincts to mate, to eat, to sleep, and to reproduce with its own kind. It is fearfully and wonderfully made.

To the untrained eye, flies are extremely clean little creatures. They land on the side of your dinner plate and immediately begin to cleanse themselves. With their front legs, they clean their eyes; then with their back legs, they carefully clean their wings and abdomen. Yes, very clean is the fly. But follow the little beast and you will find out what his appetites are really for.

To the untrained eye, man is also extremely clean. He's always washing himself in baths and showers with his many soaps and shampoos, followed up with deodorants and colognes to make him smell nice and clean. Yes, very clean is man. But follow the little beast and you will find what *his* appetites are really for. The Bible likens him to the dirty little fly by calling his spiritual father Beelzebub (meaning "Lord of the Flies"). The Scriptures say that if even the heavens are unclean in God's sight, "how much more abominable and filthy is man, who drinks iniquity like water?" (Job 15:15–16 KJV).

Here is my point. All of humanity is guilty before God. We are criminals *at fault*. All of us. "As it is written: There is none righteous, no, not one; there is none who understands; there is none who seeks after God. They have all turned aside; they have together become unprofitable; there is none who does good, no, not one" (Romans 3:10–12).

So none of us can plead innocent. We are all guilty, and here is what condemns us: "Now we know that whatever the law says, it says to those who are under the law, that every mouth may be stopped, and all the world may become guilty before God. Therefore by the deeds of the law no flesh will be justified in His sight, for by the law is the knowledge of sin" (Romans 3:18–20).

Notice that it is the "law" that brings the "knowledge of sin." In other words, God's moral law—the Ten Commandments—show us that we are criminals in God's eyes. Yet, despite our moral filthiness, God is rich in mercy and willing to cleanse us, change our appetites, and grant us everlasting life—*without* gyrations and genuflections, "Hail Marys" and "Hare Krishnas," or penance and poverty. But before that can happen, we *must* acknowledge our sins, repent, and trust the Savior, and that rarely happens until we have taken an honest look at ourselves in the light of the Ten Commandments.

So how do you stand up against God's law? Are

you innocent or guilty of breaking the Ten Commandments? How many lies do you think you have told in your life? One, two, a hundred, or have you, like most people, lost count? If you have told even one lie, you are a liar. Have you stolen anything in your life? Yes or no? Have you ever used God's name in vain, even once? Have you ever looked lusted after—or hated— anyone? If you have done these things, then you are a self-admitted lying thief, a blasphemer, an adulterer, a murderer, and a slanderer at heart. So what do you have to say for yourself? How can you justify lying, stealing, using God's name to swear, adultery, murder, and slander? Simply confessing your sins won't help you. That is like standing before a judge and just *confessing* that you are guilty as charged. How can that help? Saying you are sorry and that you won't do it again won't help either. Of course, a criminal should be sorry, and, of course, he shouldn't commit the crimes again. So what are you going to say to make things right? How can you avoid the damnation of hell?

We have already seen that any sacrifice on your part is an attempt to bribe Almighty God and pervert justice. If we stand in the presence of a holy God with only our own works, *we* will get something worse than the death sentence. We will be damned. So all we can do is raise our hands in surrender and trust in the mercy of the Judge.

Fortunately, the Bible tells us that God is "rich in mercy" (Ephesians 2:4). In the parable of the prodigal son (see Luke 15:11–32), Jesus reveals a loving father who is looking out for the return of his wayward son. Then, when he sees him, he runs to him, falls upon him, and kisses him.

You and I are the prodigal, and God is the Father. And look at what He did to save guilty sinners from damnation in hell:

> In the beginning was the Word, and the Word was with God, and the Word was God. . . . And the Word was made flesh, and dwelt among us, and we beheld his glory, the glory as of the only begotten of the Father, full of grace and truth. . . . No man hath seen God at any time, the only begotten Son, which is in the bosom of the Father, he hath declared him. . . . [And] God so loved the world, that he gave his only begotten Son, that whosoever believeth in him should not perish, but have everlasting life. (John 1:1, 14, 18; 3:16)

God the Son became a human being and suffered on *our* behalf in order to pay *our* fine, so that we could leave the courtroom! That's what took place on that terrible cross two thousand years ago (Philippians

2:8). The sin of the world fell upon the innocent Lamb of God (John 1:29)—He was bruised for *our* iniquities; by His stripes we are healed (Isaiah 53).

Notice the words "only begotten" in these verses from God's Word. They mean that Jesus was absolutely unique. He was the only One who could pay for the world's sins, because He alone was morally perfect, and He was morally perfect because He was God in human form. He proved this by raising Himself from the dead: "Therefore My Father loves Me, because I lay down My life that I may take it again. No one takes it from Me, but I lay it down of Myself. I have power to lay it down, and I have power to take it again. This command I have received from My Father" (John 10:17–18).

So what are you going to do? Are you going to stay religious, trusting in yourself, or are you going to surrender to the Savior and trust in Him alone? Everyone must make a decision about who Jesus is and whether or not he or she will submit to or reject Him. Please surrender. Do it now. Confess your sins to God and then turn from them. God will help you. And then make sure that your trust is in Jesus Christ alone. Transfer your trust from yourself to the Savior.

If you prefer to *do* something rather than trust in God's mercy, you will feel good about yourself and you will look spiritual in the eyes of this world, but all your sweat and pain will be in vain. Look at how the Bible addresses those who refuse to rely on God for salvation:

> If then you have died with Christ to material ways of looking at things and have escaped from the world's crude and elemental notions and teachings of externalism, why do you live as if you still belong to the world? [Why do you submit to rules and regulations?—such as] Do not handle [this], Do not taste [that], Do not even touch [them], referring to things all of which perish with being used. To do this is to follow human precepts and doctrines. Such [practices] have indeed the outward appearance [that popularly passes] for wisdom, in promoting self-imposed rigor of devotion and delight in self-humiliation and severity of discipline of the body, but they are of no value in checking the indulgence of the flesh (the lower nature). [Instead, they do not honor God but serve only to indulge the flesh.]" (Colossians 2:20–23 AMP)

Again, we may feel spiritual with our chanting, praying, knocking on doors, lighting candles, going on missions, etc., and we may get the world's approval for having such a show of spirituality, but using these things as a means to purchase salvation is an insult to God. It tells Him that we don't realize just how serious our crimes are. And if we can't see the seriousness of our crimes against God, we will actually believe that we can pay for them ourselves, thus earning God's favor. But the Bible even says that any sacrifice we offer Him is an abomination to Him. The word *abomination* means that they are "extremely detestable." I don't know about you, but I don't want to take any chances by offering something "extremely detestable" to try to earn a salvation that only Christ could pay for!

WHAT ABOUT REINCARNATION?

In 1968, George Harrison said, "You go on being reincarnated until you reach the actual Truth. Heaven and Hell are just a state of mind. We are all here to become Christ-like. The actual world is an illusion." He also said, "The living thing that goes on, always has been, always will be. I am not really George, but I happen to be in this body."[13]

There are, however, important questions when it comes to reincarnation. The first one is, who is in charge of giving out new bodies to everyone? It certainly isn't the God of the Bible. The Scriptures don't hint at a second chance at life. They simply say, "It is appointed unto men once to die, but after this, the judgment" (Hebrews 9:27 KJV). If there is no Judgment Day and no heaven and hell, then Hitler got away with killing six million Jews. It means that millions of killers down through the ages, who were never brought to justice, got away with murder.[14]

If God is good, He must, by nature, make sure that justice is done. If any civil judge looks the other way regarding murder, then the judge is wicked and should be brought to justice himself. A *good* judge must do everything he can to make sure that justice is done. Therefore, if God doesn't punish wickedness, then God would be evil. The exact opposite is the case. He will punish evil right down to the thoughts and intents of the heart.

Another problem with reincarnation is the standard by which we are to judge whether we come back in a good body or as a worm. Is it the Ten Commandments? Hinduism has no standard by which one can measure good and evil: "Good and evil of this world of duality are unreal, are spoken of by words, and exist only in the mind."[15]

This teaching is totally contrary to the Bible. According to the Bible, good and evil are *not* unreal (see Genesis 3:1–6, 22). Yet Sri Ramana Maharshi, a Hindu spiritual master in the early 1900s, said, "The Bible and the Gita are the same."[16]

If someone rapes your mother and slits her throat, what he did was "evil." But Hinduism says otherwise:

> Good and evil exists in our minds. That which fulfils our interests is called good, and that which brings to us misery or anything which we do not want, is called evil ... If we realize that the eternal Energy, or the Divine will, appears as good or evil only as related to our minds and lives then we can say, as the great sages in India said: "God does not create good or evil, nor does He take the virtue or sin of anybody. He does not punish the wicked or reward the virtuous. Our intelligence being covered, as it were, with the cloud of ignorance and relativity, deluded as we are, we imagine, on account of our imperfect understanding, that God creates good and evil, that His creation is good or evil, that He punishes or rewards."[17]

If the god of whom Hinduism speaks "does not punish the wicked or reward the virtuous," then that pinpoints the problem: this "god" doesn't exist. He is a figment of the human imagination, and such is a violation of the first and the second of the Ten Commandments.

George once said, "If there's a God, I want to see Him. It's pointless to believe in something without proof. Krishna consciousness and meditation are methods whereby you can actually obtain God perception."[18] The practice of Hinduism promises only a "perception" of God, but it perceives Him to be something He isn't.

Barbecue is the number-one favorite smell on many people's smell list. It brings instant salivation. The top favorite color is blue. That makes sense, because blue gives us a sense of well-being. Who doesn't appreciate a clear blue sky? What are some of the everyday pleasures you enjoy? Good music? How about the first bite of a tender steak, or some ice-cold liquid that hits the spot on a really hot day? Imagine losing all of those pleasures. Imagine if you found yourself in a place where a terrible thirst could never be quenched.

I don't need to "imagine" such a place. I am 100 percent convinced that hell exists, and hell is a place where there is no pleasure. No friends. No parties. I believe this because I know that a Creator exists. Because creation exists, it is; therefore, He does. I also know intuitively that the Creator is good, because as a man made in His image, I am part of a "moral" creation. No animal has concerns about justice and truth. Only humans. If God exists and is good, He must care about justice. *Billions* feel as I do. Simply ask any human being what God requires of us, and he or she will say that He expects us to "live a good life." From there, common sense dictates that murderers and rapists do not "live a good life," and will ultimately be punished. That's a given. But what most of humanity doesn't understand is that the *standard* of goodness that God has is infinitely higher than ours. That means that on Judgment Day, His justice will be infinitely more demanding.

To believe that God doesn't exist—that there is no absolute morality, no ultimate justice, and that you can live as you wish—is to have all your eggs in one broken-down basket with a loose handle. If you are guilty on Judgment Day, you will give up all of life's wonderful pleasures.

Think about what "damnation" actually means. Crying out, "I'm so sorry! I was wrong; God help me!" will mean nothing if you've waited too late to submit to Christ. The door of mercy will be closed. You laughed at His servants, you mocked His gospel, you blasphemed His name, you were ungrateful for the life He gave you, and you lived in a way that was abhorrent to Him. Now you must face the music. Justice will have finally caught up with you, and there will be hell to pay.

But for the Christian, hell has already been "paid." Justice has been satisfied through the suffering death of the Savior. We can leave the courtroom. We will have pleasure forevermore, on a new earth . . . one without viruses, crime, and natural disasters. God hasn't even begun to show the pleasures He has in store for those who love Him (see 2 Corinthians 2:9). We have instant salvation the moment we call upon Him, and eternal salvation awaiting us.

So, again, what's holding *you* back from repentance and faith in Jesus? Is it pride? Your love for sin? Perhaps a little of both? Maybe the next time pleasure comes your way, you will consider the sobering thoughts in this chapter. I hope so.

Newsweek magazine said of George Harrison, "His final statement, the wry, caustic *Brainwashed*, contrasts characteristically buoyant Harrison melodies with bitter commentary on media overload and narcissism. Released post-humously, the album suggests that Harrison never stopped seeking his own truth."[19]

The moment a sinner repents and trusts the One who said, "I am the truth," the seeking ends.

THE
LEGENDARY
RINGO STARR

We have got almost anything money can buy. But
when you can do that, the things you buy mean
nothing after a time. You look for something else,
for a new experience.[1]

~ *Ringo Starr*

ICHARD STARKEY, commonly known
as Ringo Starr because of the rings on his
fingers, was born on July 7, 1940, in Liverpool, England. His parents, Elsie and Richard, sepa-
rated when he was just three years old.[2]

Starkey was constantly sick as a child. At the age of six, due to complications from appendicitis, he fell into a coma for a time. When he was thirteen, he was afflicted with chronic pleurisy and spent the next two years in a sanatorium. Once he was released, he never went back to school. Later on, he developed allergies and sensitivity to food (years later, when the Beatles traveled to India, he had to take his own food).

In 1957, Starkey formed a music band with his friend Eddie Miles. Two years later, he joined the Raving Texans, and from that moment, he adopted the stage name "Ringo Starr." The following year, the group was renamed Rory Storm and the Hurricanes. While performing with them in Germany, Ringo met the Beatles.

When the Beatles decided to remove Pete Best as their drummer, Ringo joined them for his first official performance on August 18, 1962.

Because the Beatles wanted each of the band members to have a recognizable vocal personality, all four Beatles performed solos on their recordings. Ringo generally sang one song on each album. The songs, including the popular "Yellow Submarine" and "With a Little Help from My Friends," were still composed by John and Paul, but with Ringo's baritone vocal range in mind. Ringo himself composed "Don't

Pass Me By" and "Octopus's Garden."

In 1964, the day before a scheduled tour, Ringo collapsed with high fever and tonsillitis. He spent a few days in the hospital, and a replacement drummer had to be hired for the tour. Ringo rejoined the group and had his tonsils removed later that year.

Ringo married Maureen Cox in February 1965, and they had three children: Zak, Jason, and Lee.

During the *White Album* recording sessions, Ringo left the group for two weeks due to the tensions developing in the studio. John urged him to come back by sending him telegrams, and George prepared flowers for his return with the message, "Welcome home."

Ringo had technical limitations as a drummer since he was left-handed, playing a right-handed kit. Beatles producer George Martin said of him, "Ringo hit good and hard and used the tom-tom well, even though he couldn't do a roll to save his life." But in spite of Ringo's inability to "roll around the drums," as Ringo himself put it, Martin later admitted, "He's got tremendous feel. He always helped us to hit the right tempo for a song, and gave it that support— that rock-solid back-beat—that made the recording of all The Beatles' songs that much easier."[3] He was especially proud of Ringo's drumming on *Sgt.*

Pepper, stating that he was possibly the world's finest drummer. John, on the other hand, when asked if Ringo was indeed the best drummer in the world, joked, "He's not even the best drummer in The Beatles!"[4] Paul McCartney disagreed. After the band's performance on the Apple Studios' roof in 1969, Paul sent him a postcard saying, "You are the greatest drummer in the world. Really."[5]

After the Beatles breakup, Ringo released a couple of albums that included such hits as "It Don't Come Easy," "Back Off Boongaloo, "You're Sixteen," and "Photograph." He also participated in Harrison's "Concert for Bangladesh" in 1971, and played with John's Plastic Ono Band.

In 1975, after a ten-year marriage, Ringo and Maureen divorced. In spite of the split, Ringo continued to release some successful albums, including *Ringo the 4th*, and remained a celebrity, but by the end of the decade, his commercial impact had diminished.

On April 27, 1981, Ringo married actress Barbara Bach. But by October 1988, both needed to attend a detox clinic for alcoholism. Each received a six-week treatment before being released.

The following year, "Ringo Starr & His All-Starr Band" appeared in front of a ten-thousand-person audience in Dallas, Texas. Ringo's "All-Starr Band" consisted of a number of other artists who had each experienced success on their own. Together, they played well-known songs by the Beatles, by Ringo himself, and by the musicians.

In 1990, the All-Starr tour's success led Ringo to release an album with live compilations of his concerts. He released two additional albums in the 1990s and appeared as a guest on other artists' recordings, such as Paul's *Flaming Pie* in 1997.

Ringo was inducted into the Percussive Arts Society Hall of Fame in 2002. In November of the same year, at the concert for George held on the first anniversary of his death, Ringo "caught everyone with a tear in their eye with a rendition of 'Photograph,' a composition he wrote with George, which seemed to sum up how everyone felt." The lyrics say, "Every time I see your face / it reminds me of the places we used to go / But all I've got is a photograph / and I realize you're not coming back anymore."[6]

In 2007, the European edition of *Time* featured a three-page article focused on Ringo's happy life and music. The article briefly announced an upcoming album, titled *Liverpool 8.*

In early October 2008, too busy to continue signing the myriad of items fans sent to his home, he posted a video on his website saying that he wasn't going to sign any more autographs after October 20.

In February 2010, Ringo received the 2,401st star on the Hollywood Walk of Fame by the Hollywood Chamber of Commerce. It was placed in front of the Capitol Records Building along with John and George's stars.

Ringo celebrated his seventieth birthday on July 7, 2010, at Radio City Music Hall with an All-Starr Band concert. Joining him onstage were friends and family such as Yoko Ono, Paul McCartney, and his son Zak, who is also a professional drummer and former member of the band Oasis.

RINGO AND GOD

During his childhood, Ringo attended an evangelical Anglican church.[7] But did his religious upbringing impact his opinions and decisions?

Back in August 1964, while in Los Angeles, Ringo and John were asked what they thought of mixed marriages between religions. John replied first, "I would think it's up to the people concerned you know. If they can take it. It's pretty rough. It's known to be rougher over here but it's the same in England. You know, do it!"[8]

Then Ringo gave his thoughts. He said:

> I don't know, if you love a girl, say you're a—as we call them—Church of England Protestant and the girl's a Catholic as long as you love the girl and she loves you . . . the only thing is that the families get on to you. You're quite happy with the girl and then her family will start sort of picking on her, saying[,] well[,] "what are the children going to be?" or "what religion? Is he going to change for you?", and your family will say[,] "you'll never have any luck cause you're marrying a Catholic" and all that but if you're just left alone I think there'd be a lot more mixed marriages but, the thing, they break up because of the other people and they NEVER break up because of the actual pair.

Lennon added, "I got married before I even knew what religion my wife was; anyway I never asked her. I mean religion is more of a . . ."

"Personal thing," Ringo finished for him.[9]

Religion did remain a "personal thing" for Ringo right up until 2010, when he said that he had "found God." According to Ben Todd, a writer for Britain's *Daily Mail*, Ringo admitted he wasn't on the right path when he experimented with marijuana and LSD while in the Beatles, and then, in the late 1970s when he suffered with cocaine and alcohol problems. Ben Todd wrote:

But the musician, who has since become teetotal and quit his 60-a-day cigarette habit, says that religion now plays an important role in his life. Todd also reported that Ringo stated, "I feel the older I get, the more I'm learning to handle life. Being on this quest for a long time, it's all about finding yourself. For me, God is in my life. I don't hide from that. I think the search has been on since the 1960s. . . . I stepped off the path there for many years and found my way back onto it, thank God.[10]

Steve Turner, author of *The Gospel According to The Beatles*, said that when he wrote that book, "Ringo had an album with a track called 'Oh My Lord' on it which was very gospelly sounding and didn't refer to Krishna." Turner also said:

He's certainly changed from the old days when he didn't care about religion at all—not even much for TM (Transcendental Meditation). If you remember, he was first out of the meditation camp . . . As a child he attended an Anglican church near his home which had an evangelical tradition, but only because they had nice toys at Sunday school and you got paid to sing in the choir! Of course I hope that he has had a true conversion but I always fear that it's just another love-peace-togetherness and a-higher-power kind of thing. I think I sent him a copy of my book when it was published but I might now send it again.[11]

Referring to his upcoming birthday, Ringo told the *LA Times* that it was far easier approaching seventy than approaching forty: "'Forty was: Oh, God, 40!' he said. 'There's that damn song, "Life Begins at 40." No, it's not so big anymore. I am nearly 70, and I'd love to be nearly 40, but that's never going to happen.'"[12]

A Christian may fall at times into sin, but we should be deeply concerned about the genuineness of someone's faith when we see him thank God, and in the next breath, not only use His name in vain, but also curse.

It isn't uncommon for celebrities (or anyone for that matter), as they grow older, to think more about their own mortality. However, there is a huge difference between an intellectual admission that God exists, and actually obeying Him. Look at what the Bible says about Jesus and the part of obedience in salvation:

> . . . who, in the days of His flesh, when He had offered up prayers and supplications, with vehement cries and tears to Him who was able to save Him from death, and was heard *because of His godly fear*, though He was a Son, yet He learned obedience by the things which He suffered. And having been perfected, He became the author of eternal salvation to all who obey Him. (Hebrews 5:7–9; emphasis added)

Notice also that Jesus was heard by God because He had a "godly fear." Someone who has a godly fear would never use God's name carelessly. Look at what Scripture further says about this subject and notice its use of the word *fear*: "He has not dealt with us according to our sins, nor punished us according to our iniquities. For as the heavens are high above the earth, *so great is His mercy toward those who fear Him;* as far as the east is from the west, so far has He removed our transgressions from us. As a father pities his children, *so the Lord pities those who fear Him*" (Psalm 103:10–13; emphasis added).

If our sins have been forgiven, we will fear God. Arguably, the number one reason so many lack the fear of God is that they have never been confronted with God's moral law. They've never understood the great biblical truth that we are criminals in the sight of a holy God. We have violated His law by lying, stealing, blaspheming, lusting, showing ingratitude, committing adultery/fornication, and more. Unforgiven, we are guilty, condemned to death, and will eventually be locked in God's prison—a place called "hell"—without any chance of parole. The biblical word for that is "damned." What a fearful thing.

There is a principle in criminal law called *mens rea* (Latin for "guilty mind"). The term itself means "criminal intent" and is one of several elements of a crime that must be established beyond a reasonable doubt to prove criminal liability.[13] In other words, if a man commits rape or murder, the question is asked as to whether or not he knew at that time that what he was doing was morally wrong. If so, that establishes the case for his prosecution.

Who of us doesn't have a "guilty mind" when it comes to lying, stealing, adultery, blasphemy, and murder? This is because "the work of the Law" (Romans 2:15) is written upon our hearts and minds. The effect of the presence of the knowledge of right and wrong is that the conscience will accuse us of guilt. The Amplified Bible puts it this way: "They show that the essential requirements of the Law are written in their hearts and are operating there, with which their consciences (sense of right and wrong) also bear witness; and their [moral] decisions (their arguments of reason, their condemning or approving thoughts) will accuse or perhaps defend and excuse [them]" (Romans 2:15 AMP).

For many, the feeling of guilt is nothing more than an annoyance, to be shaken off like an annoying bug on the hand. Bug us though it may, the function of the conscience is similar to that of a smoke detector, and that feeling of guilt is its alarm.

The sound of a smoke detector's alarm may be annoying, but we appreciate it because of its function. Its very *purpose* is to be annoying, because it wants to alarm us about imminent danger.

That's the function of the alarm of the conscience. Each time you hear it, it's saying there is imminent danger, and that danger is the Day of Judgment, when the fire of God's indignation will rage against all evil, and any violation of the perfect law of God is evil in His holy eyes.

If you remove the batteries from a smoke detector because you don't like the grating alarm, and the consequence is that you lose your life in a fire, people will say that you were a fool. The tragedy is that sometimes entire families perish because of an irresponsible father who has done that very thing. The same case applies to the voice of the human conscience and the salvation of God.

There is something else in criminal law that is extremely important to understand. It is *Ignorantia juris non excusat*—from the Latin "ignorance of the law does not excuse." This legal principle means that even though a person is unaware of a law, he or she is still liable for its violation. So the one who breaks that law is guilty even though he or she wasn't aware of the law's content. If you drive through a country town at 80 miles per hour, ignorant of the fact that the town's law says 50 miles per hour is the maximum speed, you are still guilty of a speeding violation and held accountable.

Being held accountable for violating a law of which you had no knowledge may seem unreasonable, because there is no way any one person could be aware of every law on the books. However, the purpose of this principle is to ensure that "willful blindness" cannot become the basis of a plea of innocence. Such is the case with the willful ignorance of those who profess to be atheists—"I didn't believe; therefore I am guiltless." The law of God still condemns its violators, despite willful ignorance—what the Bible calls "unbelief."

However, a good judge will take *genuine* ignorance into account. This is the case with God because He's rich in mercy toward those who fear Him. Even though you have intuitive knowledge that adultery is a violation of God's moral Law, you may be ignorant of the fact that He considers lust to be adultery (Matthew 5:27–28). Or, even though you may think it's okay to have a personal conception of God (either as an image of wood, or as an image in your mind), you may not be aware that this is a violation of the second of the Ten Commandments. Before anyone carves an idol, he conceives the image in his mind—the place of imagery. Most in America don't go so far as to carve a physical image of their god in wood or in stone, but their *image* of God is idolatrous. He is seen as a divine butler or a celestial Santa Claus.

The Apostle Paul says that covetousness (violation of the Tenth Commandment—a sin of the heart) is idolatry:

"Mortify therefore your members which are upon the earth; fornication, uncleanness, inordinate affection, evil concupiscence, and covetousness, which is idolatry" (Colossians 3:5).

This was the sin of the rich young ruler (see Mark 10:17). God was not first in his affections. His god was his money.

"You shall not make for yourself a carved image—any likeness of anything that is in heaven above, or that is in the earth beneath, or that is in the water under the earth; you shall not bow down to them nor serve them" (Exodus 20:4).

The first commandment says, "You shall have no other gods before Me" (v. 1) However, this is not a passive commandment. It doesn't just mean that God, the Giver of life, should be first in our affections. It means much more than that. The "before Me," means "before my face." In other words, the veneration of false gods—whether carved from wood and stone or nurtured in the imagination of this sinful world, printed, and sold for a profit—is not immaterial to Him. Idolatry is in His face. It's an offense to God. It angers Him, and for good reason. Inordinate affection tends to stir emotions, even in human beings. No parent wants his or her child to love a gift given to him more than he loves the one who gave the gift.

But idolatry carries with it even more than inordinate affection. Making up a false god opens the door to violation of the other nine commandments. For example, a man will not give himself to adultery or murder if he has a correct understanding of the nature and power of God. Knowledge tends to help us govern our decisions. Any wide-eyed imbecile may hold on to a lighted stick of dynamite, but a man who understands what he holds in his hand will make sure he is a good distance from a lighter.

And so a man who has the knowledge that the eye of the Lord is in every place, beholding the evil and the good, will separate himself quickly from the sin of adultery. He knows that he is accountable to God for every word, every thought, and every deed, and therefore a healthy fear of God keeps him from sin—and it will keep him out of hell.

But the idolater's image of God doesn't produce

the fear of God. To him, God is a friend, a buddy, or a divine butler who doesn't mind lust or adultery. So the idolater doesn't depart from sin, because he doesn't fear God, and therefore his sin will take him to hell. Idolatry is not just an offense in the face of God; it also brings terrible and eternal consequences.

When the apostle Paul arrived in the city of Athens, the Bible tells us that he was grieved because the city had given itself to idolatry. In their ignorance, they had done what most civilizations do: they had made God to be as they imagined Him to be. Paul said,

> Therefore, the One whom you worship without knowing, Him I proclaim to you: God, who made the world and everything in it, since He is Lord of heaven and earth, does not dwell in temples made with hands. Nor is He worshiped with men's hands, as though He needed anything, since He gives to all life, breath, and all things. And He has made from one blood every nation of men to dwell on all the face of the earth, and has determined their preappointed times and the boundaries of their dwellings, so that they should seek the Lord, in the hope that they might grope for Him and find Him, though He is not far from each one of us; for in Him we live and move and have our being, as also some of your own poets have said, "For we are also His offspring." (Acts 17:23–28)

How foreign these words are even to modern "traditional" Christianity. Many whisper when they enter a building they call a "church" because they assume that that is where God dwells. But the Scriptures tell us that God "does not dwell in temples made with hands." He is as much in your home as He is at places we assume are holy, and He is nothing like we conceive Him to be.

After Paul proclaimed to the Greeks who God *really* was, then the apostle gave them the good news that even though they were guilty of violating the second of the Ten Commandments, God would overlook their ignorance:

> Therefore, since we are the offspring of God, we ought not to think that the Divine Nature is like gold or silver or stone, something shaped by art and man's devising. *Truly, these times of ignorance God overlooked,* but now commands all men everywhere to repent, because He has appointed a day on which He will judge the world in righteousness by the Man whom He has ordained. He has given assurance of this to all by raising Him from the dead. (vv. 29–31; emphasis added)

If you have suddenly realized that you have also been guilty of creating a god in your own image, the

Bible has the same message for you. You must repent because God has appointed a fearful Day of Judgment, and the only way to be safe on that Day is to trust in the Savior, Jesus Christ. Maybe you're a skeptic, or you think that "religion is a personal thing." Maybe you have made it through this book, but you still lack a fear of God. Then let me tell you about someone I knew who lacked a healthy fear of God.

When I preached the gospel in the city of Christchurch, New Zealand, almost every day for twelve years, a man named Willie heckled me almost daily for years. He would mock me, curse me, curse my children, and angrily spit venom at God. Here is what I wrote about him:

"ODE TO WILLIE"

Let me tell you about Willie, a non-Christian friend

How his heckling of my preaching, came to an end

He said if God was real, he'd spit in His face

When Willie was angry, I would always give him space.

There were times I would think that he had no brain

Or at least I thought, he must be partly insane

He would look at the heavens and yell "God strike me dead!"

Because if God did exist, He would do what he said.

One day God graciously answered his prayer

And I have to tell you, that Willie's no longer here

It wasn't lightning that came from the sky

But an attack on his heart, that caused Willie to die.

He was just a young man when death came his way

And if he could speak now, I know what he'd say

Where Willie went I really don't know

But I do know there's a place you don't want to go.

If he didn't trust Jesus, please don't follow Willie

He would tell you to listen and not to be silly

Maybe you peeked behind the atheist door

And you widened your eyes at what you then saw.

There was lust, and sex, and a whole lot of porn

So much pleasure, you thanked God you were born

You think about life, and your longing to sin

And you think about Heaven and your chance
to get in

You think about God, the Bible and Hell
You think about Willie and what he would yell
You think about Jesus and what He did for you
You think about the things you'd so love to do.

What a big problem you have with your sin
What a dilemma you find yourself in
What can you do, so you won't feel so bad?
What can you do to make your heart glad?

There's an easy solution, if you just want *this* life
But it's kind of like cutting your throat with a
knife
You would simply believe that everything evolved
You just have to stop thinking, and the problem
is solved.

The Beatles once professed to be atheists, but
then soon abandoned such a thoughtless worldview.
As they matured, each of them began to think about
the precious miracle of life, and what really matters.

It's my hope that George and John found the
Savior. God only knows what happened just before

they passed from this life. Special though these four men may have been to you and me, the Beatles were no more special to God than any other four individuals that He created. The Bible tells us that He is "no respecter of persons." On Judgment Day, our fame, talent, or how much we have in the bank will be meaningless. All that will matter is: are we right with God? Are our sins forgiven, or are we still under the wrath of God's law? So forget about everyone and everything for a moment, and think very seriously about your own eternal salvation. Think about your many sins, and think about the Savior and what He did for you on that cross . . . Now, confess your sins to God, turn from them in repentance, and then surrender to Jesus Christ. Don't put it off. You may not have tomorrow.

There's a YouTube clip that breaks my heart. During a Paul McCartney solo rendition of "All My Loving," the camera pans the ecstatic fans that are bursting with joy at what they are seeing and hearing.[14] In the middle of the joy is one distraught man, with a pained look on his face, weeping openly. If you have never experienced OBN (Overwhelming Beatle Nostalgia), I can't explain it to you. But I can let you know that I'm a chronic sufferer. Even while researching for this book, reading just the titles of early Beatles songs brought me close to tears.

The first time I saw that weeping man, I so empathized with him I wanted to hug him and say, "I know why you are crying!" The overwhelming emotion is tied into memories that can never be regained, and a crushing sense of helpless futility because they are fading and will soon be gone forever.

The empathy makes me want to find him and make sure that he has found the consolation of the gospel—that he has found the bedrock of salvation in the quicksand of this life's futility. Perhaps I will never meet him and plead with him to fall at the foot of the cross, but I can plead with you through the pages of this book.

An atheist once said that John Lennon's famous song "Imagine" is an "anthem for atheism." But think about it for a moment. If I said, "Imagine there's no New York, it's easy if you try," I'm saying that New York is a real place, but let's imagine (or pretend) that it isn't. So the song is actually acknowledging the existence of Heaven and Hell as real places. The realities of Heaven or Hell don't disappear just because we imagine that they don't exist.

In a 1980 interview with Playboy magazine, just months before he died, John explained what he had in mind when he composed "Imagine." He said, "It is the concept of positive prayer ... If you can imagine a world at peace, with no denominations of religion—not without religion but without this my-God-is-bigger-than-your-God thing—then it can be true."[15]

Even though John Lennon's religious views may have varied over the years, it seems that his real contention may not have been with Heaven or Hell (whatever he may have conceived them to be), or with countries or religion, possessions or wars, but rather with wicked people who cause wars over possessions and countries, in the name of their religion.

Whatever the case, the time will come when God Himself will stop all evil—and will usher in the reality where "the world will live as one." Make sure you are part of that coming kingdom—where peace will have a chance, and where God's will, will be done on earth as it is in Heaven. Millions of us are waiting for the day when the lion will lie down with the lamb. I hope someday you'll join us. Even better, I hope today you'll join us, because, as John said in his last interview, tomorrow only comes for us if God is willing. John Lennon having passed into eternity, now knows more than ever that Heaven and Hell are not imaginary; and from there he would plead with you, to not miss out on Heaven.

Don't miss "Genius"— the fascinating documentary on the life of John Lennon: **Genius-TheMovie.com**

Lennon-McCartney Timeline [1]

July 6, 1957. Paul McCartney, fifteen, is introduced to John Lennon, who is sixteen.

October 18, 1957. Paul McCartney appears from the first time with the Quarrymen (also written as the "Quarry Men") as they perform at New Clubmoor Hall in Liverpool. John and Paul start writing songs together.

April 24, 1960. John and Paul perform at the Fox and Hounds Pub in Caversham, Berkshire, and they appear for the second and last time as the Nerk Twins.

October 1, 1961. Lennon and McCartney fly to Paris for a vacation. There they meet with a friend from Hamburg, Jurgen Vollmer, who convinces them to change their hairstyles to the "mop top" worn in France at that time.

January 1, 1962. The Beatles audition for Decca Records with three Lennon-McCartney songs: "Hello Little Girl," "Love of the Loved," and "Like Dreamers Do."

June 6, 1962. First recording session at Abbey Road Studios in London for the Beatles' EMI/Parlophone audition. They record: "Besame Mucho," "Love Me Do," "P.S. I Love You," and "Ask Me Why."

November 26, 1962. The Beatles record their second single.

January 26, 1963. Performance at King's Hall, Stoke-on-Trent, Staffordshire: John and Paul compose the song "Misery" while waiting backstage. They want to donate that song to Helen Shapiro, whom they will meet in a few days.

February 19, 1963. The song "Please Please Me" is the first Lennon-McCartney song to go to the number one spot in the charts.

February 28, 1963. While riding on a bus, Paul and John compose what will be their third single, "From Me to You."

April 3, 1963. Performance at the Playhouse Theatre in London: the Beatles record three songs for the BBC radio show *Easy Beat*.

April 4, 1963. The Beatles record a third radio program for the BBC program *Side by Side*. This will mark the only recording of their song "I'll Be On My Way." As Paul finishes writing this song, John writes "Do You Want to Know a Secret?"

June 26, 1963. The Beatles perform at the Majestic Ballroom, Newcastle-upon-Tyne. Later in their hotel room, John and Paul compose "She Loves You."

June 27, 1963. Billy J. Kramer & the Dakotas record two Lennon-McCartney songs, "Bad to Me" and "I Call Your Name."

July 24, 1963. The Fourmost records the Lennon-McCartney song "Hello Little Girl."

September 10, 1963. The song "I Wanna Be Your Man" is given to the Rolling Stones to record. (It will make it into the Top 20.)

September 27, 1963. Paul's song "Love of the Loved" is released in the UK but will make it only to the Top 30. This is one of Paul's first songs and has been part of the Beatles' repertoire since the Quarrymen days.

October 3, 1963. Vocals for the song "Little Child" are overdubbed.

November 1, 1963. The Rolling Stones single "I Wanna Be Your Man," penned by Lennon-McCartney, is released.

November 15, 1963. The Fourmost release the single "I'm in Love," by Lennon-McCartney.

December 27, 1963. John Lennon and Paul McCartney are named "Outstanding Composers of 1963" by the London *Times*.

December 29, 1963. John and Paul are named the "greatest composers since Beethoven" by the London *Sunday Times*. John Lennon's book *In His Own Write* is published.

April 4, 1964. The top five positions on the American singles chart are occupied by Lennon-McCartney songs.

April 16, 1964. The Beatles record "A Hard Day's Night," which they composed beginning with the title, and then the lyrics, not the usual way.

June 2, 1964. The Beatles record several songs at Studio Two, EMI Studios in London.

February 18, 1965. The song "You've Got to Hide Your Love Away" is recorded.

February 19, 1965. The Beatles record "You're Going to Lose That Girl," in one day for the upcoming album *Help!*

April 13, 1965. The first day of filming for *Help!* is completed. The Beatles begin recording the song of the same name.

May 9, 1965. The Beatles attend a Bob Dylan concert and are impressed by his music, especially John and George.

June 14, 1965. Paul begins recording "Yesterday" and the group records "I've Just Seen a Face."

June 15, 1965. "It's Only Love" is recorded in six takes.

June 24, 1965. *A Spaniard in the Works*, John Lennon's second book, is published in the UK by Jonathan Cape.

July 1, 1965. *A Spaniard in the Works* is published in the United States by Simon and Schuster.

September 10, 1965. The Silkie, another group managed by Brian Epstein, releases the Lennon-McCartney song "You've Got to Hide Your Love Away."

October 12, 1965. The Beatles start the recording sessions for the album *Rubber Soul*, later considered a masterpiece.

October 18, 1965. The Beatles complete the recording of George's song "If I Needed Someone."

October 21, 1965. Recording begins for the song "Nowhere Man." Improvements are made to "Norwegian Wood (This Bird Has Flown)."

October 24, 1965. The Beatles spend the whole day working on "I'm Looking Through You."

November 1, 1965. The Beatles rehearse and film for a TV special titled "The Music of Lennon & McCartney."

November 2, 1965. Second day of filming for the TV special.

November 3, 1965. The Beatles spend nine hours recording "Michelle."

November 11, 1965. The group is in the recording studio completing the recordings of Paul's "You Won't See Me" and John's "Girl."

December 1965. Paul records a Christmas record called *Paul's Christmas Album* and gives one copy to each member of the band. (Only four copies are made.) *McCall's* magazine prints John's poem "Toy Boy."

April 14, 1966. Using all the technology available at that time, the Beatles record John's "Rain."

May 12, 1966. Three songs for the album *Revolver* are mixed.

June 15, 1966. The album *Yesterday and Today* is released.

June 21, 1966. The Beatles spend the day in the recording studio recording, from start to finish, John's song "She Said, She Said."

August 6, 1966. John and Paul record a BBC radio program at Paul's home.

September 5, 1966. John Lennon flies to Celle, West Germany, to start filming the movie, *How I Won the War*, a film by Richard Lester.

September 18, 1966. Beatles road manager Neil Aspinall travels with John from West Germany to Carboneras, Spain, the main location for the movie *How I Won the War.*

November 1966. John records four demos of his song "Strawberry Fields Forever."

November 24, 1966. The Beatles get together to record their new album. The first song is "Strawberry Fields Forever," with John's memories and LSD elements.

December 18, 1966. The movie *The Family Way*, with music from Paul, premieres in London.

December 29, 1966. Recording of Paul's "Penny Lane" begins.

January 5, 1967. The Beatles spend the day in the recording studio working on songs such as "Penny Lane" and "Revolution 9."

February 17, 1967. The Beatles begin recording "Being for the Benefit of Mr. Kite!" a song based almost entirely on an old circus advertising poster.

March 11, 1967. Grammy awards are given to the Beatles: Song of the Year for "Michelle," Best Solo Vocal Performance to Paul for "Eleanor Rigby," and Best Album Cover to Klaus Voorman for *Revolver.*

March 20, 1967. John and Paul record and interview with British broadcaster Brian Matthew. They make clear that there won't be any more Beatles tours.

May 17, 1967. The Beatles begin recording John's "You Know My Name (Look Up the Number)." The song will not be released until March 1970.

May 18, 1967. The announcement is made that the Beatles have been chosen to represent the UK in the first worldwide satellite program. The group meets to compose special songs for the event.

August 22, 1967. The band records Paul's song "Your Mother Should Know."

September 5, 1967. The band records "I Am the Walrus," which requires sixteen takes to complete.

September 8, 1967. The instrumental song "Flying" is recorded. This is the first instrumental song since 1961's "Cry for a Shadow."

October 12, 1967. The Beatles go to the Abbey Road Studio to record a session of *Magical Mystery Tour.* John takes on the role of producer.

November 10, 1967. Three color promos for the new single "Hello Goodbye" are filmed; direction is taken by Paul McCartney.

February 6, 1968. Ringo Starr appears on the BBC1 program *Cilla*, hosted by singer-actress Cilla Black.

May 1968. John's girlfriend, Yoko Ono, encourages John to expand his creativity beyond the Beatles. (The group has begun to resent Yoko's presence and John's rapidly decreasing interest in the Beatles.)

May 14, 1968. John and Paul announce that their newly created company, Apple, wants to help emerging artists.

May 20, 1968. After their visit to India, the Beatles have several new songs that will be included on the *"White Album."*

July 26, 1968. John goes to Paul's house to collaborate and to finish their next single, "Hey Jude."

September 23, 1968. The Beatles record forty-five takes of "Happiness Is a Warm Gun."

October 11, 1968. Paul McCartney uses the pseudonym "Apollo C. Vermouth" and produces the single "I'm the Urban Spaceman" for the group Bonzo Dog Band.

March, 1969. Twenty-three percent of shares from Northern Songs, a music public company founded by Dick James, Brian Epstein, John, and Paul, are sold by Dick James, without the Beatles' knowledge, to Associated Television. (Paul secretly buys shares and ends up with 100,000 more than John. This contributes to the friction between them.)

April 30, 1969. John and Paul (without George and Ringo) finish the vocals and effects for the song "You Know My Name (Look Up the Number)."

May 5, 1969. Associated Television acquires control over Northern Songs and the Lennon-McCartney catalog.

June, 1969. John and Yoko hold a "Bed-In" in Montreal, Canada, and record "Give Peace a Chance."

August 1, 1969. The Beatles record sixteen takes for the song "Because."

Mid-September 1969. John wants to quit The Beatles but doesn't announce it because of legal ties with EMI.

September 25, 1969. John and Paul lose control over their song catalog.

April 10, 1970. Paul announces publicly that he is leaving the Beatles and will release his first solo album, *McCartney*.

August 1970. Paul writes to John, trying to arrange the legal breakup of the band.

December 1970. Paul files a suit against Beatles & Co. to officially dissolve the group's partnership and complete the breakup.

December 4, 1971. John severely criticizes Paul publicly, ensuring that a Beatles reunion will never be possible.

October 24, 1979. *The Guinness Book of World Records* honors Paul McCartney as the most successful composer and recording artist of all time.

November 1980. John records a demo of "Dear John," perhaps the last song he ever recorded. It will never be released.

December 8, 1980. John Lennon is murdered. Yoko Ono calls for an international silent tribute.

October 11, 1982. The album *20 Greatest Hits* is released.

November 15, 1988. *The Beatles Box Set* is released.

November 21, 1995. Apple Records releases the Beatles' compilation album *Anthology 1*, the first in a three-volume collection.

March 1996. Apple releases *Anthology 2*.

October 1996. Apple releases *Anthology 3*.

December 7, 2009. *The Beatles Stereo Box Set* USB flash drive is released in the UK.

November 16, 2010. The Beatles' music catalog is released on iTunes.

Beatles Trivia

In the final song of their 1963 album, "Please Please Me," when singing twist and shout, John so pushed his voice to its limit that weeks later, he said it still felt like sandpaper.

John said of McCartney's "All My Loving," he was jealous he hadn't written it himself.

The title, "A Hard Day's Night," came from Ringo, when he used the phrase after a long work day.

Paul McCartney's, "Yesterday," has had more than 1,600 recorded versions, making it the most recorded song in music history.

"I Want to Hold Your Hand," was not only their first U.S. number one hit, but it became their best-selling worldwide single.

Before Paul settled on the name, "Eleanor Rigby," he used the phrase, "Dazzi-de-da-zu" as a filler.

The song, "Strawberry Fields Forever," was inspired by a Salvation Army house near the young John Lennon's childhood home.

The Guinness Books of Records calls Paul McCartney, "the most successful musician and composer in popular music history."

Over the eight years they worked together, the Beatles produced twelve albums, more than two hundred songs, including twenty-seven number-one hits, and sold more than 600 million albums worldwide.

SAVE YOURSELF SOME PAIN

HELPFUL PRINCIPLES FOR NEW CHRISTIANS

*I*T IS MY SINCERE HOPE that you have made peace with God through trusting in Jesus Christ. Becoming a Christian is the most incredible event that will ever take place in your life. If you have obeyed the gospel by turning from your sins and placing your trust in Jesus Christ alone for your salvation, *you have found everlasting life*! (See John 3:16; Romans 6:23; 10:9–13; 1 John 5:11–13.) Be assured, God will never leave you nor forsake you (Hebrews 13:5). He has brought you this far, and He will complete the wonderful work He has begun in you (Philippians 1:6). He knows your every thought, your every care, and your deepest concerns.

Let's look at some of those possible concerns. First, and of primary concern, do you have "assurance" of your salvation? The Bible says to "make every effort to confirm your calling and election" (2 Peter 1:10 HCSB), so let's go through a short checklist to make sure you are truly saved:

❐ Are you aware that God became flesh in the person of Jesus Christ (1 Timothy 3:16), and that He died for the sins of the world?

❐ Did you come to the Savior because you knew you had sinned against God?

❐ Are you convinced that Jesus suffered and died on the cross for your sins, and that He rose again on the third day?

❐ Did you truly "repent" (turn from your sin) and put your faith (trust) in Jesus?

God acquits us from the Courtroom of Eternal Justice on the grounds that Jesus Christ paid our fine. We are "justified" (made right with God) by His suffering death. The resurrection of Jesus Christ was God's seal of approval signifying that His precious blood was sufficient to pay the fine. If we turn from sin and place our trust in Jesus—the only grounds for forgiveness—God will grant us mercy. However, if you're not sure of your salvation, read Psalm 51 and make it your own prayer.

Following are several important principles that can save you a great deal of pain.

1. Feeding on the Word—Daily Nutrition

A healthy baby has a healthy appetite. If you have truly been "born" of the Spirit of God, you will have a healthy appetite. The Bible says, "Like newborn infants, desire the unadulterated spiritual milk, so that you may grow by it in [your] salvation" (1 Peter 2:2 HCSB). So feed yourself daily without fail. The more you eat, the quicker you will grow, and the less bruising you will have. Speed up the process and save yourself some pain—vow to read God's Word every day, without fail. Job said, "I have treasured the words of His mouth more than my daily food" (Job 23:12 HCSB). Be like Job, and put your Bible *before* your belly. Say to yourself, "No Bible, no breakfast. No read, no feed." If you do that, God promises that you will be like a fruitful, strong, and healthy tree (see Psalm 1).

Each day, find somewhere quiet and thoroughly soak your soul in the Word of God. There may be times when you read through its pages with great enthusiasm, and other times when it seems dry and even boring. But food profits your body whether you enjoy it or not. As a child, you no doubt ate desserts with great enthusiasm. Perhaps vegetables weren't so exciting. If you were a normal child, you probably had to be encouraged to eat them at first. Then, as you matured in life, you learned to discipline yourself to eat vegetables. This is because they nourish and strengthen you, even though they may not bring pleasure to your taste buds.

2. Faith—Elevators Can Let You Down

When a young man once said to me, "Ray, I find it hard to believe some of the things in the Bible," I smiled and asked, "What's your name?" When he said, "Paul," I casually answered, "I don't believe you." He looked at me questioningly. I repeated, "What's your name?" Again he said, "Paul," and again I answered, "I don't believe you." Then I asked, "Where do you live?" When he told me, I said, "I don't believe that either." His reaction, understandably, was anger. I said, "You look a little upset. Do you know why? You're upset because I didn't believe what you told me. If you tell me that your name is Paul, and I say, 'I don't believe you,' it means that I think you are a liar. You are trying to deceive me by telling me your name is Paul, when it's not."

Then I told him that if he, a mere man, felt insulted by my lack of faith in his word, how much more does he insult Almighty God by refusing to believe His Word? In doing so, he was saying that God isn't worth trusting—that He is a liar and a deceiver. The Bible says, "The one who does not believe God has made Him a liar" (1 John 5:10 HCSB). It also says, "Watch out, brothers, so that there won't be in any of you an evil, unbelieving heart" (Hebrews 3:12 HCSB). Martin Luther said, "What greater insult . . . can there be to God, than not to believe His promises?"

I have heard people say, "But I just find it hard to have faith," not realizing the implications of their words. These are the same people who often accept the daily weather forecast, believe the newspapers, and trust their lives to a pilot they have never seen whenever they board a plane. We exercise faith every day. We rely on our car's brakes. We trust history books, medical books, and elevators. Yet planes can crash. History books can be wrong. Elevators can let us down. How much more, then, should we trust the sure and true promises of Almighty God. He will never let us down . . . if we trust Him.

Cynics often argue, "You can't trust the Bible— it's full of mistakes." It is. The first mistake was when man rejected God, and the Scriptures show men and women making the same tragic mistake again and again. It's also full of what *seem* to be contradictions. For example, the Scriptures tell us that "nothing will be impossible with God" (Luke 1:37 HCBS), in other words, there is nothing Almighty God cannot do. Yet we are also told that it is "impossible for God to lie" (Hebrews 6:18). So there *is* something God cannot do! Isn't that an obvious "mistake" in the Bible?

The answer to this dilemma is found in the lowly worm.

Do you know that it would be impossible for me to eat worms? I once saw a man on TV butter his toast, then pour on a can of live, fat, wriggling, blood-filled worms. He carefully took a knife and fork, cut into his moving meal, and ate it. It made me feel sick. It was disgusting. The thought of chewing cold, live worms is so repulsive, so distasteful, I can candidly say that it would be *impossible* for me to eat them, even though I have seen it done. It is so abhorrent, I draw on the strength of the word "impossible" to substantiate my claim.

Lying, deception, bearing false witness, however you want to phrase it, is so repulsive to God, so disgusting to Him, so against His holy character, that the Scriptures draw on the strength of the word "impossible" to substantiate the claim. He cannot, could not, and would not lie.

That means that in a world where we are continually let down, we can totally rely on, trust in, and count on His promises. They are sure, certain, indisputable, true, trustworthy, reliable, faithful, unfailing, dependable, steadfast—an anchor for the soul. In other words, you can truly believe them, and because of that, you can throw yourself blindfolded and without reserve into His mighty hands. He will never, *ever* let you down. Do you believe that?

3. Evangelism—Our Most Sobering Task

Late in December 1996, a large family gathered in Los Angeles for a joyous Christmas. There were so many gathered that night, five of the children slept in the converted garage, kept warm during the night by an electric heater placed near the door.

During the early hours of the morning, the heater

suddenly burst into flames, blocking the doorway. In seconds, the room became a blazing inferno. A frantic 911 call revealed the unspeakable terror, as one of the children could be heard screaming, "I'M ON FIRE!" The distraught father vainly rushed into the flames to try to save his beloved children, receiving burns to 50 percent of his body. Tragically, all five children burned to death. They died because steel bars on the windows had thwarted their escape. There was only one door, and it was blocked by the flames.

Imagine you are back in time, just minutes before the heater burst into flames. You peer through the darkness at the peaceful sight of five sleeping youngsters, knowing that at any moment, the room will erupt into an inferno and burn the flesh of horrified children. *Can you in good conscience walk away?* No! You *must* awaken them, and warn them to run from that death trap!

The world sleeps peacefully in the darkness of ignorance. There is only one Door by which they may escape death. The steel bars of sin prevent their salvation, and at the same time, call for the flames of eternal justice. What a fearful thing Judgment Day will be! The fires of the wrath of Almighty God will burn for eternity. The Church has been entrusted with the task of awakening the lost before it's too late.

We cannot turn our backs and walk away in complacency. Think of how the father *ran* into the flames. His love knew no bounds. Our devotion to the sober task God has given us will be in direct proportion to our love for the lost. There are only a few laborers who run headlong into the flames to warn them to flee (Luke 10:2). *Please* be one of them. We really have no choice. The apostle Paul said, "Woe is me if I do not preach the gospel!" (1 Corinthians 9:16).

If you and I ignore a drowning child and let him die when we had the ability to save him, we are guilty of the crime of depraved indifference. God forbid that any Christian should be guilty of that crime when it comes to those around us who are perishing. We have an obligation to reach out to them. The "Prince of Preachers," Charles Spurgeon, said, "Have you no wish for others to be saved? Then you are not saved yourself. Be sure of that." A Christian *cannot* be apathetic about the salvation of the world. The love of God in him will motivate him to seek and save that which is lost.

You probably have a limited amount of time after your conversion to impact your unsaved friends and family with the gospel. After the initial shock of your conversion, they will put you in a neat little ribbon-tied box and keep you at arm's length. So it's important that you take advantage of the short time you have while you still have their ears.

Here's some advice that may save you a great deal of grief. As a new Christian, I did almost irreparable damage by acting like a wild bull in a crystal showroom. I bullied my mom, my dad, and many of my friends into making a "decision for Christ." I was sincere, zealous, loving, kind, and stupid. I didn't understand that salvation doesn't come through making a "decision," but through *repentance*, and that repentance is God-given (2 Timothy 2:25). The Bible teaches that no one can come to the Son unless the Father "draws" him (John 6:44). If you are able to get a "decision" but the person has no conviction of sin, you will almost certainly end up with a stillborn on your hands.

In my "zeal without knowledge" I actually inoculated the very ones I was so desperately trying to reach. There is nothing more important to you than the salvation of your loved ones, and you don't want to blow it. If you do, you may find that you don't have a second chance. Fervently pray for them, asking God for their salvation. Let them *see* your faith. Let them *feel* your kindness, your genuine love, and your gentleness. Buy gifts for no reason. Do chores when you are not asked to. Go the extra mile. Put yourself in their position. You know that you have found everlasting life—*death has lost its sting!* Your joy is unspeakable. But as far as they are concerned, you've been brainwashed and have become part of a weird sect. So your loving actions will speak more loudly than ten thousand eloquent sermons.

For this reason, you should avoid *verbal* confrontation until you have knowledge that will guide your zeal. Pray for wisdom and for sensitivity to God's timing. You may have only one shot, so make it count. Keep your cool. If you don't, you may end up with a lifetime of regret. *Believe* me. It is better to hear a loved one or a close friend say, "Tell me about your faith in Jesus Christ," than for you to say, "Sit down. I want to talk to you." Continue to persevere in prayer for those you love, that God would open their eyes to the truth.

Remember also that you have the sobering responsibility of speaking to other people's loved ones. Perhaps another Christian has prayed earnestly that God would use a faithful witness to speak to his beloved mom or dad, and *you* are that answer to prayer. You are the true and faithful witness God wants to use. We should share our faith with others *whenever* we can. The Bible says that we should proclaim the message and "persist in it whether convenient or not" (2 Timothy 4:2 HCSB).

Never lose sight of the world and all its pains. Keep the fate of the ungodly before your eyes. Too many of us settle down on a padded pew and become introverted. Our world becomes a monastery without walls. Our friends are confined solely to those *within* the Church, when Jesus was the friend of sinners (see Luke 15:2). So take the time to deliberately befriend the lost for the sake of their salvation. Remember that each and every person who dies in his sins has an appointment with the Judge of the universe. Hell opens wide its terrible jaws. There is no more sobering task than to be entrusted with the gospel of salvation—working with God for the eternal well-being of dying humanity. Have the same attitude as the apostle Paul, who pleaded for prayer for his own personal witness. He said, "Pray also for me, that the message may be given to me when I open my mouth to make known with boldness the mystery of the gospel. For this I am an ambassador in chains. Pray that I might be bold enough in Him to speak as I should" (Ephesians 6:19–20 HCSB).

4. Prayer—"Wait for a Minute"

God always answers prayer. Sometimes He says yes; sometimes He says no; and sometimes He says, "Wait for a minute." And since God is outside the dimension of time, to Him, a thousand years is no different than a day (see 2 Peter 3:8)—which could mean a ten-year wait for us. So ask in faith, but rest in peace-filled patience.

Surveys show that more than 90 percent of Americans pray daily.[1] No doubt they pray for health, wealth, happiness, etc. They also pray when Grandma gets sick, so when Grandma doesn't get better (or dies), many end up disillusioned or bitter. This is because they don't understand what the Bible says about prayer. It teaches, among other things, that our sin will keep God from even hearing our prayers (Psalm 66:18), and that if we pray with doubt, we should not even expect to get an answer (James 1:6–7). Here's how to be heard:

- Pray with faith (Hebrews 11:6).

- Pray with clean hands and a pure heart (Psalm 24:3–4).

- Pray genuine, heartfelt prayers, rather than vain repetitions (Matthew 6:7).

- Make sure you are praying to the God revealed in the Holy Scriptures (Exodus 20:3–6).

How do you "pray with faith"? Someone once said to me, "Ray, you're a man of great faith in God," thinking that he was paying me a compliment. But he wasn't—the compliment was to God. For example, if I said, "I'm a man of great faith in my doctor," it's actually the doctor I'm complimenting. If I have great faith in him, it means that I see him as being a man of integrity, a man of great ability—that he is trustworthy. I give "glory" to the man through my faith in him. The Bible says that Abraham "did not waver in unbelief at God's promise, but was strengthened in his faith and gave glory to God, because he was fully convinced that what He had promised He was also able to perform" (Romans 4:20–21 HCSB). Abraham was a man of great faith in God. Remember, that is not a compliment to Abraham. He merely caught a glimpse of God's incredible ability, His impeccable integrity, and His wonderful faithfulness to keep every promise He makes. Abraham's faith gave "glory" to a faithful God.

As far as God is concerned, if you belong to Jesus, you are a VIP. You can boldly come before the throne of grace (Hebrews 4:16). You have access to the King because *you are the son or daughter of the King.* When you were a child, did you have to grovel to get your needs met by your mom or dad? I hope not.

So, when you pray, don't say, "Oh, God, I *hope* you will supply my needs." Instead say something like, "Father, thank You for keeping every promise You make. Your Word says that you will supply *all* my needs according to Your riches in glory in Christ Jesus [Philippians 4:19], so today I am asking for [make your request] in the wonderful name of Jesus, and I thank You in advance for doing this thing. Amen." (See how Jesus prayed in John 11:42.)

The great missionary Hudson Taylor said, "The prayer power has never been tried to its full capacity. If we want to see Divine power wrought in the place of weakness, failure, and disappointment, let us answer God's standing challenge [from Jeremiah 33:3], 'Call unto me, and I will answer thee, and show thee great and mighty things which thou knowest not (KJV).'"

How do you get "clean hands and a pure heart"? Simply by confessing your sins to God, through Jesus Christ, whose blood cleanses us from all our sin (see 1 John 1:7–9). Not only will God *forgive* your every sin; He promises to *forget* them (Hebrews 8:12). He will count it as though you had never sinned in the first place. He will make you pure in His sight—sinless. He will even "purge your conscience" (Hebrews 9:14 KJV), so that you will no longer have a sense of guilt over your sin. That's why you need to soak yourself in Holy Scripture; read the letters to the churches and see the wonderful things God has done for us through the cross of Calvary. If you don't bother to read the "will," you won't have any idea what has been given to you.

How do you pray "genuine heartfelt prayers"? Simply by keeping yourself in the love of God. If the love of God is in you, you will never pray hypocritical or selfish prayers. In fact, you won't have to pray selfish prayers if you have a heart of love, because when your prayer life is pleasing to God, He will reward you openly (see Matthew 6:6). Just talk to your heavenly Father as candidly and intimately as a young child, nestled on Daddy's lap, would talk to his earthly father. How would you feel if every day your child pulled out a prewritten statement to dryly recite to you, rather than pouring out the events and emotions of that day? God wants to hear from your heart.

How do you know you're praying to "the God revealed in Scripture"? Study the Bible. Don't accept the image of God portrayed by the world, even though it appeals to the natural mind. A gentle, kind, Santa Claus figure, dispensing good things but with no sense of justice or truth, appeals to guilty sinners. Look to the thunderings and lightnings of Mount Sinai (Exodus 20:18). Gaze at Jesus on the cross of Calvary—hanging in unspeakable agony because of the justice of a holy God (Romans 1:18–20). Such thoughts tend to banish idolatry.

5. Warfare—Praise the Lord and Pass the Ammunition

When you became a Christian, you stepped right into the heat of an age-old battle. You now have a three-fold enemy: the world, the flesh, and the Devil. Let's look at these three resistant enemies.

Our first enemy is the "world." This refers to the sinful, rebellious world system. The world loves the darkness and hates the light (John 3:20), and is governed by the "prince of the power of the air" (Ephesians 2:2). The Bible says that the Christian has escaped the corruption that is in the world through lust. "Lust" is unlawful desire, and is the lifeblood of the world—whether it be lust for sexual sin, for power, for money, or for material things. Lust is a monster that will never be gratified, so don't feed it. It will grow bigger and bigger until it weighs heavy upon your back, and will be the death of you (James 1:15).

There is nothing wrong with sex, power, money, or possessions, but when the desire for these becomes predominant, it becomes idolatry (Colossians 3:5). We are told, "Do not love the world or the things that belong to the world. If anyone loves the world, love for the Father is not in him," and, "Whoever wants to be the world's friend becomes God's enemy" (1 John 2:15; James 4:4 HCSB).

The second enemy is the Devil, who is the "god of this age" (2 Corinthians 4:4 HCSB). He was your spiritual father before you joined the family of God (John 8:44; Ephesians 2:2). Jesus called the Devil a thief who came to steal, kill, and destroy (John 10:10). The way to overcome him and his demons is to make sure you are outfitted with the spiritual armor of God listed in Ephesians 6:10–18. Become intimately familiar with it. Sleep in it. Never take it off. Bind the sword to your hand so you never lose its grip. The reason for this brings us to the third enemy.

The third enemy is what the Bible calls the "flesh." This is your sinful nature. The domain for the battle is your mind. *If you have a mind to*, you *will* be attracted to the world and all its sin. The mind is the control panel for the eyes and the ears, the center of your appetites. All sin begins in the "heart" (Proverbs 4:23; Matthew 15:19), which refers to your mind. We think of sin before we commit it. James 1:15 warns that lust, once conceived, brings forth sin, and sin, if allowed to develop, brings forth death. Every day of life, we have a choice. To sin or not to sin—that is the question. The answer rightly is to have the fear of God. If you don't fear God, you will sin to your sinful heart's delight.

Speaking of the fear of God, did you know that God kills people? He killed a man for what he did sexually (Genesis 38:9–10), killed another for being greedy (Luke 12:15–21), and killed a husband and wife for telling one lie (Acts 5:1–10). Knowledge of God's goodness—His righteous judgments against evil—should put the fear of God in us and help us not to indulge in sin.

If we know that the eye of the Lord is in every place, beholding the evil and the good, and that He will bring every work to judgment, we will live accordingly. Such weighty thoughts are valuable, for "one turns from evil by the fear of the LORD" (Proverbs 16:6 HCSB). Jesus said, "And I say to you, My friends, don't fear those who kill the body, and after that can do nothing more. But I will show you the One to fear: Fear Him who has authority to throw [people] into hell after death. Yes, I say to you, this is the One to fear!" (Luke 12:4–5 HCSB).

6. Fellowship—Flutter by, Butterfly

Pray about where you should fellowship. Make sure the place you select as your church home calls sin what it is—sin. Does the congregation believe the promises of God? Are they loving? Does the pastor treat his wife with respect? Is he a man of the Word? Does he have a humble heart and a gentle spirit? Listen closely to his teaching. It should glorify God, magnify Jesus, and edify the believer.

One evidence that you have been truly saved is that you will have a love for other Christians (1 John 3:14). You will want to fellowship with them. The old saying that "birds of a feather flock together" should be especially true of Christians. You gather together for the breaking of bread (communion), for teaching from the Word, and for fellowship. You share the same inspirations, illuminations, inclinations, temptations, aspirations, motivations, and perspirations—you are working together for the same thing: the furtherance of the kingdom of God on earth. This is why you attend church—not because you have to, but because you want to.

Don't become a "spiritual butterfly." If you are

flitting from church to church, how will your pastor know what type of food you are digesting? The Bible says that your shepherd is accountable to God for you (Hebrews 13:17), so make yourself known to your pastor. Pray for him regularly. Pray also for his wife, his family, and the church leaders. Being a pastor is no easy task. Most people don't realize how long it takes to prepare a fresh sermon each week. They don't appreciate the time spent in prayer and in the study of the Word. If the pastor repeats a joke or a story, remember: he's human. So give him a great deal of grace and double honor. Never murmur about him. If you don't like something he has said, pray about it, then leave the issue with God. If that doesn't satisfy you, leave the church, rather than divide it through murmuring and complaining. God hates those who cause division among believers (Proverbs 6:16–19).

7. Thanksgiving—Do the Right Thing

For the Christian, every day should be "Thanksgiving Day." We should be thankful even in the midst of problems. The apostle Paul said, "I am overcome with joy in all our afflictions" (2 Corinthians 7:4 HCSB). He knew that God was working all things together for his good, even his trials (Romans 8:28).

Problems *will* come your way. God will see to it personally that you grow as a Christian. He will allow storms in your life in order to send your roots deep into the soil of His Word. We also pray more in the midst of problems. It's been well said that you will see more from your knees than on your tiptoes.

A man once watched a butterfly struggling to get out of its cocoon. In an effort to help it, he took a razor blade and carefully slit the edge of the cocoon. The butterfly escaped from its problem . . . but immediately died. It is God's way to have the butterfly struggle. It is the struggle that causes its tiny heart to beat fast, sending lifeblood into its wings.

Trials have their purpose. They are a cocoon in which we often find ourselves. They make us struggle—they bring us to our knees. It is there that the lifeblood of faith in God helps us spread our wings.

Faith and thanksgiving are close friends. If you have faith in God, you will be thankful because you know His loving hand is upon you, even though you are in a lion's den. That will give you a deep sense of joy, which is the barometer of the depth of faith you have in God. Let me give you an example.

Imagine if I said I'd give you one million dollars if you sent me an e-mail. Of course, you don't believe I would do that. But imagine if you did, and that you knew a thousand people who had each sent me an e-mail, and every one received their million dollars—no strings attached. More than that, you actually called me, and I assured you personally that I would keep my word. If you believed me, wouldn't you have joy? If you didn't believe me—no joy. The amount of joy you have would be a barometer of how much you believed my promise.

We have so much for which to be thankful. God has given us "exceedingly great and precious promises" (2 Peter 1:4 KJV). Do yourself a big favor: believe them, thank God continually for them, and let your joy "be full" (see John 15:11).

8. Water Baptism—Sprinkle or Immerse?

The Bible says, "Repent . . . and be baptized, each of you, in the name of Jesus Christ for the forgiveness of your sins" (Acts 2:38 HCSB). There is no question about whether you should be baptized. The questions are, how, when, and by whom?

It would seem clear from Scripture that those who were baptized in Bible times were fully immersed in water. Here's one reason why: "John also was baptizing in Aenon near Salim, because there was plenty of water there" (John 3:23 HCSB). If John were merely sprinkling believers, he would have needed only a cupful of water. Baptism by immersion pictures our death to sin, our burial with Christ, and our resurrection to new life in Him (see Romans 6:4, Colossians 2:12).

The Philippian jailer and his family were baptized at midnight, the same hour they believed (Acts 16:30–33). The Ethiopian eunuch was baptized as soon as he believed (Acts 8:35–37), as was Paul (Acts 9:17–18). Baptism is a step of obedience, and God blesses our obedience. So what are you waiting for?

Who should baptize you? It is clear from Scripture that other believers had the privilege, but check with your pastor; he may want the honor himself.

9. Tithing—The Final Frontier

It has been said that the wallet is the "final frontier." It is the final area to be conquered—the last thing that we surrender to God. Jesus spoke much about money. He said that we cannot serve both God and mammon (Matthew 6:24). The word used for "money" was the common Aramaic word for riches, which is related to a Hebrew word signifying "that which is to be trusted." In other words, we cannot trust God and money. Either money is our source of joy, our great love, our sense of security, the supplier of our needs—or God is.

When you open your purse or wallet, give generously and regularly to your local church. A guide to how much you should give can be found in the "tithe" of the Old Testament: 10 percent of your income (Genesis 14:20). Whatever amount you give, make sure you give *something* to the work of God (see Malachi 3:8–11). Give because you want to, not because you have to. God loves a cheerful giver (2 Corinthians 9:6–7), so learn to hold your money with a loose hand.

10. Troubleshooting—Cults, Atheists, and Skeptics
If you know the Lord, nothing will shake your faith. It is true that the man with an experience is not at the mercy of a man with an argument. If you are converted, and the Holy Spirit "testifies" that you are a child of God (Romans 8:16 HCSB), you will never be shaken by a skeptic.

When cults tell you that to be saved you must call God by a certain name, you must worship on a certain day, or that you must be baptized by an elder of his church, don't panic. Merely go back to the Instruction Manual. The Bible has all the answers, and searching them out will make you grow. If you feel intimidated by atheists—if you think they are "intellectuals"—read my book *God Doesn't Believe in Atheists*. It will reveal that they are the opposite. It will also show you how to *prove* God's existence, and also prove that the "atheist" doesn't exist. (See also *How to Know God Exists*, another of my books.)

The way to prevent sporting injuries and pain is to keep yourself fit through exercise. The apostle Paul kept fit through exercise. He said, "Herein do I exercise myself, to always have a conscience void of offence toward God, and toward men" (Acts 24:16 KJV). Do the same. Listen to the voice of your conscience. It's your friend, not your enemy. Remember the words of Solomon: "Fear God and keep His commands, because this is for all humanity. For God will bring every act to judgment, including every hidden thing, whether good or evil" (Ecclesiastes 12:13–14 HCSB).

Keep the Day of Judgment before your eyes. On that Day, you will be glad you cultivated a tender conscience. I hope these principles have been helpful and that they will someday save you some pain.

Feel free to check out our website, www.livingwaters. com, where you will discover helpful books (*The Way of the Master* is our most important publication); DVDs; unique gospel tracts; free audio and video messages (make sure you listen to "Hell's Best Kept Secret," and then "True and False Conversion"); an online Bible School with more than 12,000 online students; an exciting Academy; details of our award-winning television program *The Way of the Master*; the daily online broadcast; information on our "Transformed" and "Deeper" conferences; and many other materials to help you grow in your faith.

Notes

CHAPTER 1

1. *Skiffle* is a type of music having blues, jazz, roots, and folk influences and often using improvised instruments, such as washboards and jugs. The term itself originated in the United States in the early 1900s, and the genre was popular in the U.S. from the 1920s to the 1940s. Skiffle regained popularity when it experienced a revival in Great Britain in the 1950s.
2. *Fete* is a French word meaning "festival" or "party." In English, it is used now as a label for certain events, particularly outdoor entertainment.
3. A *tea chest bass* is a stringed instrument built from a wooden case called a *tea chest*, used to ship tea to the UK. Similar to a washtub bass, the instrument is played by plucking strings on a broomstick or other type of pole. The tea chest itself increases the resonance of the tones produced when strings are plucked.
4. http://beatlesnumber9.com/quarrymen.html.
5. http://beatlesquotes.com/paul-mccartney-quotes.htm.
6. Sutcliffe died a few months later, due to a brain hemorrhage. See *Wikipedia*, s.v., "The Beatles," http://en.wikipedia.org/wiki/Beatle. Much of the historical content of this chapter is drawn from this article.
7. *Wikipedia*, s.v. "Brian Epstein," http://en.wikipedia.org/wiki/Brian_Epstein.
8. The Beatles, *The Beatles Anthology* (San Francisco: Chronicle, 2000), 68.

9. *Wikipedia*, s.v. "Brian Epstein," http://en.wikipedia.org/wiki/Brian_Epstein.

10. "The Lennon-McCartney Songwriting Partnership," http://h2g2.com/dna/h2g2/A5950929.

11. Interview in London, Heathrow Airport, 8:10 a.m., Saturday, February 22, 1964, http://www.britishpathe.com/video/beatles-welcome-home/query/Heathrow.

12. Albert Hofmann, *LSD: My Problem Child* (Sarasota, FL: Multidisciplinary Association for Psychedelic Studies [MAPS], 2005), 47.

13. Ibid.

14. Ibid., 47–50.

15. DEA Public Affairs, "DEA—Publications—LSD in the US—The Drug," November 16, 2001.

16. *Wikipedia*, s.v., "History of Lysergic Acid Diethylamide," http://en.m.wikipedia.org/wiki/History_of_LSD.

17. *Wikipedia*, s.v., "Lucy in the Sky with Diamonds," http://en.wikipedia.org/wiki/Lucy_in_the_Sky_with_Diamonds.

18. Ibid.

19. Caroline Goddard, "Beatles' Muse Lucy Vodden Dies," *She Knows Entertainment*, September 28, 2009, http://www.sheknows.com/entertainment/articles/811261/beatles-muse-lucy-vodden-dies.

20. Peter Wilkinson, "'Lucy in the Sky with Diamonds' Dies," *CNN.com*, September 29, 2009, http://edition.cnn.com/2009/SHOWBIZ/Music/09/29/beatles.lucy.in.the.sky.with.diamonds/index.html.

21. http://entertainment.timesonline.co.uk/tol/arts_and_entertainment/music/beatles/article6820697.ece.

22. http://www.songfacts.com/detail.php?id=120.

23. The Beatles Ultimate Experience, http://www.beatlesinterviews.org/dbjypb.int3.html.

24. Jennifer Berube, "The Truth Behind the Beatles Song Lucy in the Sky with Diamonds," July 13, 2010, http://50s-60s-pop-music.suite101.com/article.cfm/the-truth-behind-the-beatles-song-lucy-in-the-sky-with-diamonds.

25. *Wikipedia*, "Lucy in the Sky with Diamonds."

26. *Wikipedia*, "The Beatles."

27. http://www.besteveralbums.com/overall.php. *Sgt. Pepper* places number five on this list of "best ever albums," on the "overall chart."

28. Anthony Barnes, "Where's Adolf? The Mystery of Sgt. Pepper Is Solved," *Belfast Telegraph* (Ireland), February 5, 2007, http://www.belfasttelegraph.co.uk/entertainment/music/news/wheres-adolf-the-mystery-of-sgt-pepper-is-solved-13411115.html.

29. Barry Miles, *Many Years from Now* (Vintage-Random House, 1997), 405.

30. *The Beatles Anthology* (DVD) 2003, episode 1.

31. Interview available at http://www.whale.to/b/lennon1.html.

32. The Beatles, *The Beatles Anthology*, 237.

CHAPTER 2

1. John Lennon, "Beautiful Boy," © EMI Music Publishing, Sony/ATV Music Publishing LLC.

2. Geoffrey Giuliano, *Lennon in America: 1971–1980, Based in Part on the Lost Lennon Diaries* (Cooper Square Press, 2001), 17.

3. Timothy White, Rock Lives: Profiles and Interviews (Holt Paperbacks, 1991), 114.

4. Peter Brown, *The Love You Make: An Insider's Story of The Beatles* (New York: McGraw Hill, 1983), 222.

5. Maureen Cleave, "How Does a Beatle Live? John Lennon Lives Like This," *London Evening Standard*, March 4, 1966, http://headsup.freeshell.org/beatles-articles/standard.html.

6. Ibid.

7. http://www.onthemedia.org/yore/transcripts/transcripts_020604_mania.html. Site no longer accessible.

8. James R. Gaines, "Descent into Madness: The Life and Crime of Mark David Chapman," *People*, June 22, 1981, http://www.people.com/people/archive/article/0,,20079581,00.html.

9. *Wikipedia*, s.v., "More Popular Than Jesus," http://en.wikipedia.org/wiki/More_popular_than_Jesus. You can see this interview at "The Beatles http://www.youtube.com/watch?v=WZt67ceN03Y.

10. "Author: The Beatles Were a 'Spiritual Force,'" November 26, 2008, http://edition.cnn.com/2008/SHOWBIZ/Music/11/25/pope.beatles/.

11. Ibid.

12. "We Are Bigger Than Jesus," http://www.youtube.com/watch?v=LhpyxoOeYGY, applicable part starts at the 00:53 mark.

13. "Playboy Interview: John Lennon and Yoko Ono."

CHAPTER 3

1. http://johnlennonquotes.net/john-lennon-political-and-religion-quotes.htm.

2. "The Beatles Playboy Magazine Interview: February 1965," http://
   archives.absoluteelsewhere.net/TextArchive/BeatlesArchives/
   beatles_playboy_int_65.html.
3. http://johnlennonquotes.net/john-lennon-political-and-religion-
   quotes.htm.
4. The Beatles, *The Beatles Anthology*, 226.
5. Jonathan Wynne-Jones, "Bigger Than Jesus? The Beatles Were a Christian Band," *The Telegraph*, July 12, 2008, http://www.telegraph.
   co.uk/news/uknews/2403617/Bigger-than-Jesus-The-Beatles-were-
   a-Christian-band.html.
6. Ibid.
7. Ibid.

CHAPTER 4

1. *The Way of the Master* is aired in seventy countries.
2. Lennon-McCartney, "Yesterday," 1965.
3. http://www.poodwaddle.com/worldclock.swf. No longer accessible.
4. *John Lennon Anthology*, CD #3: *The Lost Weekend*," track #20, "Phil
   and John 3." (Phil Spector, born Harvey Philip Spector, is an
   American songwriter and record producer. Spector, who came up
   with the music production technique known as the "wall of sound,"
   pioneered the 1960s girl-group sound and produced more than
   twenty-five Top 40 hits between 1960 and 1965. Later in his career,
   he worked with such artists as George Harrison, John Lennon, the
   Ramones, and Ike and Tina Turner, with parallel success. For more,
   see the *Wikipedia* article "Phil Spector" at http://en.wikipedia.org/
   wiki/Phil_Spector.)
5. "Elton John Tried to Commit Suicide," August 15, 2007, http://www.
   exposay.com/elton-john-tried-to-commit-suicide/v/13071/.
6. The 2003 shooting death of actress Lana Clarkson in his Alhambra,
   California, home led to his being charged with murder in the
   second degree. After a 2007 mistrial, he was convicted in 2009
   and given a prison sentence of nineteen years to life.
7. Interview with RKO Radio on the day of his murder (December 8,
   1980).
8. Bible commentator Matthew Henry wrote of these verses: "We are
   dying creatures, all our comforts in the world are dying comforts,
   but God is an ever-living God, and believers find him so. When
   God, by sickness, or other afflictions, turns men to destruction, he
   thereby calls men to return unto him to repent of their sins, and live

a new life. A thousand years are nothing to God's eternity: between a minute and a million of years there is some proportion; between time and eternity there is none. All the events of a thousand years, whether past or to come, are more present to the Eternal Mind, than what was done in the last hour is to us. And in the resurrection, the body and soul shall both return and be united again. Time passes unobserved by us, as with men asleep; and when it is past, it is as nothing. It is a short and quickly-passing life, as the waters of a flood. Man does but flourish as the grass, which, when the winter of old age comes, will wither; but he may be mown down by disease or disaster." (*Matthew Henry's Concise Commentary on the Bible*, http://mhc.biblecommenter.com/psalms/90.htm.)

CHAPTER 5

1. The Beatles Ultimate Experience: Beatles Interviews Database: John Lennon & Yoko Ono Interview: Apple Offices, London 5/8/1969, http://www.beatlesinterviews.org/db1969.0508.beatles.html.

2. Giuliano, *Lennon in America*, 2.

3. Davies, *The Beatles.*

4. Giuliano, *Lennon in America*, 2.

5. *Rolling Stone*, January 7, 1971, 39.

6. David A. Noebel, *The Marxist Minstrels: A Handbook on Communist Subversion of Music* (American Christian College Press, 1974), 111.

7. *The Schools Wikipedia*, s.v., "John Lennon," http://schools-wikipedia. org/wp/j/John_Lennon.htm.

8. *Penthouse*, October 1969, 29.

9. R. Gary Patterson, *Hellhounds on Their Trail: Tales from the Rock N Roll Graveyard* (Nashville: Dowling Press, 1997), 181.

10. *Song Magazine*, February 1984, 16.

11. Robert Rosen, *Nowhere Man* (Oakland, CA: Quick American Archives, 2002), 38.

12. Ibid., 61.

13. Giuliano, *Lennon in America*, 119, 208.

14. Ibid., 157.

15. Ibid., 81.

16. Ibid., 20.

17. Ibid., 16.

18. Ibid.

19. Ibid., 20.

20. Ibid., 111, 138.

21. Ibid., 18.
22. Ibid., 122.
23. Ibid., 142.
24. Ibid., 177.
25. Ibid., 130.
26. http://www.cardiophile.com/defibrillators.

CHAPTER 6

1. "Playboy Interview: John Lennon and Yoko Ono," reprinted from
   Playboy magazine, January 1981, http://www.recmusicbeatles.
   com/public/files/bbs/jl_yo.playboy/lennon1.html; http://www.
   quoteland.com/author/John-Lennon-Quotes/247/.
2. http://en.wikipedia.org/wiki/File:Lennon_and_Chapman.jpg.
3. BBC News, "John Lennon Killer 'Wanted Fame,'" October 15, 2004,
   http://news.bbc.co.uk/2/hi/entertainment/3745492.stm.
4. BBC News, "Mark Chapman: Destined for Infamy," October 9, 2002,
   http://news.bbc.co.uk/2/hi/entertainment/2310873.stm.
5. *Wikipedia*, s.v., "Death of John Lennon," http://en.wikipedia.org/
   wiki/Death_of_John_Lennon. Most of this chapter's account of
   Lennon's death is gleaned from this article.
6.
7. BBC News, December 8, 1980, at http://www.johnlennon.talktalk.
   net/lennon.html.
8. "Playboy Interview," 1.
9. Chris Kokenes, "Man Who Murdered John Lennon Up for Parole
   Again," *CNN.com*, July 27, 2010, http://edition.cnn.com/2010/
   CRIME/07/27/new.york.chapman.parole.hearing/index.
   html?hpt=C1#fbid=YvP-bowHa9M.
10. See Ray Comfort, *Hitler, God, and the Bible*, WND Books).
11. *Larry King Live*, "A Look Back at Mark David Chapman in His Own
    Words" (transcript), September 30, 2000, http://transcripts.cnn.
    com/TRANSCRIPTS/0009/30/lklw.00.html.

CHAPTER 7

1. Lennon-McCartney, "All You Need Is Love," 1967.
2. Ray Comfort, *Words of Comfort* (blog), "Amazing Scrapbook," November 5, 2010, http://raycomfortfood.blogspot.
   com/2010_11_01_archive.html.
3.
4. http://johnlennonquotes.net/john-lennon-political-and-religion-
   quotes.htm.

CHAPTER 8

1. http://johnlennonquotes.net/.

2. http://www.opposingviews.com/i/quelling-the-revolution-neutral-izing-john-lennon.

3. http://books.google.fr/books?id=55v1oXZwvMEC&pg=PT560&lpg=PT560&dq=according+to+biographer+Bill+Harry,+the+production+of+The+Irish+Tapes,+a+pro-IRA+documentary&source=bl&ots=siR5QBhz_2&sig=q7detc1c_7WRMzNOgvAvWGBhkGg&hl=en&sa=X&ei=eACGT5fwD4_J8gPnpajBBw&redir_esc=y#v=onepage&q=according%20to%20biographer%20Bill%20Harry%2C%20the%20production%20of%20The%20Irish%20Tapes%2C%20a%20pro-IRA%20documentary&f=false

4. "John Lennon, the FBI, and Me," http://www.guardian.co.uk/commentisfree/2006/dec/20/johnlennonthefbiandme

5. *Wikipedia*, s.v., "*The U.S. vs. John Lennon*," http://en.wikipedia.org/wiki/The_U.S._vs._John_Lennon.

6. Transcript from the documentary film titled The U.S. vs. John Lennon, quoted in "EXCLUSIVE: Yoko Ono on the New Imagine Peace Tower in Iceland, Art & Politics, the Peace Movement, Government Surveillance and the Murder of John Lennon," *Democracy Now!* October 16, 2007, http://www.democracynow.org/2007/10/16/exclusive_yoko_ono_on_the_new.

7. "BBC interview with John Lennon and Victor Spinetti," June 6, 1968, http://www.beatlesbible.com/1968/06/06/bbc-interview-with-john-lennon-and-victor-spinetti/.

8. *Wikipedia*, s.v., "John Lennon," http://en.wikipedia.org/wiki/John_Lennon.

9. Harold Lepidus, "Bob Dylan and John Lennon—Part Four," *Bob Dylan Examiner*, October 8, 2010, http://www.examiner.com/bob-dylan-in-national/bob-dylan-and-john-lennon-part-four?render=print.

10. *Wikipedia*, s.v., "Nutopia," http://en.wikipedia.org/wiki/Nutopia.

11. *Wikipedia*, "John Lennon."

12. *Wikipedia*, s.v., "Jon Wiener," http://en.wikipedia.org/wiki/Jon_Wiener.

13. "Sir Paul McCartney Denies He Did Not Get on With John Lennon," *Telegraph* (London), August 25, 2009, http://www.telegraph.co.uk/culture/music/music-news/6083346/Sir-Paul-McCartney-denies-he-did-not-get-on-with-John-Lennon.

14. DS INTERVIEW: Alistair Begg on Spirituality of the Beatles, http://www.dickstaub.com/culturewatch.php?record_id=360. No longer

accessible.

15. Ibid. Also at http://culturesphere.org/culturewatch.php?record_id=360.

16. "*Playboy* Interview."

17. John Lennon, in "Music: John Lennon," The Quote Cache, http://quotes.prolix.nu/Authors/?John_Lennon; http://quotes.prolix.nu/Music/John_Lennon/.

18. Rosen, *Nowhere Man*; Giuliano, *Lennon in America*.

19. Giuliano, *Lennon in America*, 133.

20. Ibid., 134.

21. John Lennon, "Serve Yourself," at Sing365.com, http://www.sing365.com/music/lyric.nsf/Serve-Yourself-lyrics-John-Lennon/6B40790 90B32203A48256BCA000A6CE3.

22. Steve Turner, "The Ballad of John and Jesus," *Christianity Today*, June 12, 2000, 86.

CHAPTER 9

1. *Wikipedia*, s.v., "Mark David Chapman," http://en.wikipedia.org/wiki/Mark_David_Chapman.

2. James R. Gaines, "Mark Chapman: The Man Who Shot Lennon," *People*, February 23, 1987.

3. Fred McGunagle, *Mark David Chapman: The Man Who Killed John Lennon*, chap. 3, "A Troubled Youth," at TruTV Crime Library, http://www.trutv.com/library/crime/terrorists_spies/assassins/chapman/3.html.

4. "Descent Into Madness," *People*, June 22, 1981, vol. 15, no. 24, http://www.people.com/people/archive/article/0,,20079581,00.html.

5. *Wikipedia*, s.v., "Mark David Chapman," http://en.wikipedia.org/wiki/Mark_David_Chapman.

6. Kristina Jones, "Banned Book: *The Catcher in the Rye*," March 7, 2007, http://voices.yahoo.com/banned-book-catcher-rye-224799.html.

7. McGunagle, *Mark David Chapman*, chap. 6, "To the Brink and Back," http://www.trutv.com/library/crime/terrorists_spies/assassins/chapman/6.html.

8. *Wikipedia*, s.v., "Cultural References to the Novel *The Catcher in the Rye*," http://en.wikipedia.org/wiki/Cultural_references_to_the_novel_The_Catcher_in_the_Rye.

9. McGunagle, *Mark David Chapman*, chap. 7, "Is That All You Want?" http://www.trutv.com/library/crime/terrorists_spies/assassins/chapman/7.html.

10. Gaines, "Descent into Madness."
11. Ibid.
12. Ibid.
13. *Wikipedia*, "Mark David Chapman."
14. Ibid.
15. Ibid.
16. Jonathan Wald, "Lennon Killer Denied Parole," October 6, 2004, CNN Justice, http://articles.cnn.com/2004-10-05/justice/chapman.parole_1_extreme-malicious-intent-lennon-killer-attica-correctional?_s=PM:LAW.
17. *Wikipedia*, "Mark David Chapman."
18. "Lennon Killer Denied Parole," BBC News, October 3, 2000, http://news.bbc.co.uk/2/hi/americas/955074.stm.
19. BBC News, "Mark Chapman: Destined for Infamy," October 6, 2004, http://news.bbc.co.uk/2/hi/entertainment/3719204.stm.
20. *Wikipedia*, "Mark David Chapman."
21. Lynne H. Schultz, "March 4th, 1966: The Beginning of the End for John Lennon?" http://www.infidels.org/kiosk/article73.html.
22. *Wikipedia*, "Mark David Chapman."
23. Schultz, "March 4th, 1996."
24. Ibid.
25. *Wikipedia*, "Mark David Chapman."

CHAPTER 10

1. John Lennon, as quoted in a BBC interview with David Wigg, May 8, 1969.
2. Gaines, "Descent into Madness."
3. Ray Comfort, *God Has a Wonderful Plan for Your Life: The Myth of the Modern Message* (Living Waters, 2010). See www.FreeWonderfulBook.com.
4. See Acts 8:59–60.
5. Gaines, "Descent into Madness."
6. "A Look Back at Mark David Chapman in His Own Words."
7. McGunagle, *Mark David Chapman*, chap. 7.
8. Michael Ellison, "Lennon's Killer Applies for Parole," *Guardian* (UK), September 4, 2000, http://www.guardian.co.uk/uk/2000/sep/05/michaelellison.
9. "Mark David Chapman Explains Motivation behind John Lennon Murder," *Telegraph*, September 17, 2010, http://www.telegraph.co.uk/culture/music/the-beatles/8008098/Mark-David-Chapman-

explains-motivation-behind-John-Lennon-murder.html.

10. Ibid.

11. Michael S. James, "John Lennon Killer Also Considered Shooting Johnny Carson, Elizabeth Taylor," September 6, 2012, http://abcnews.go.com/Entertainment/john-lennon-killer-mark-david-chapman-considered-killing/story?id=11658475#.T4YEO-1MbVU.

12. The lyrics that follow are from John Lennon's, "Imagine," recorded and released in 1971. The full lyrics are available at http://www.lyrics.com/imagine-lyrics-john-lennon.html. Lyrics quoted for educational purposes, under the "Fair Use" law: FL 102, Fair Use, and Circular 21, Reproductions of Copyrighted Works by Educators and Librarians.

13. "And I will say to my soul, 'Soul, you have many goods laid up for many years; take your ease; eat, drink, and be merry.' But God said to him, 'Fool! This night your soul will be required of you; then whose will those things be which you have provided?' So is he who lays up treasure for himself, and is not rich toward God" (Luke 12:19–21).

CHAPTER 11

1. http://beatlesquotes.com/paul-mccartney-quotes.htm.

2. Gilbert Garcia, "The Ballad of Paul and Yoko," January 27, 2003, Salon.com, http://www.salon.com/2003/01/27/paul_yoko/.

3. Bill Harry, *The Beatles Encyclopedia*, 2000 paperback ed. (London: Virgin Publishing, 2000), 403.

4. "The Story of Linda McCartney," http://beatlesnumber9.com/linda.html.

5. "Hurray! Knighthood for Paul McCartney," http://mcbeatle.de/macca/knight.html.

6. "Biography of Paul McCartney, IMDB, http://www.imdb.com/name/nm0005200/bio.

7. *Wikipedia.com*, s.v., "Paul McCartney," http://en.wikipedia.org/wiki/Sir_Paul_McCartney.

8. "Yesterday" has had more than three thousand covers recorded by many artists.

9. "Paul McCartney," http://www.worldtop.org/Culture/People/Most+influential+people+ever/Paul+McCartney/.

CHAPTER 12

1. Paul McCartney Trivia and Quotes, http://www.tv.com/paul-mccartney/person/3548/trivia.html.

2. Miles, *Many Years from Now*, 9.

3. "Let It Be." Lyrics quoted for educational purposes, under the "Fair Use" law: FL 102, Fair Use, and Circular 21, Reproductions of Copyrighted Works by Educators and Librarians.

4. *Wikipedia*, "Let It Be (song)," http://en.wikipedia.org/wiki/Let_It_Be_(song).

5. John M. Whitehead, "With Father's Day Approaching, Paul McCartney Reminisces about Dad," *Opinion* by Rutherford Institute.

6. "John Lennon: The New Jesus?" http://beatlesnumber9.com/jesuslennon.html.

7. Ibid.

8. "Paul McCartney: Getting Better All the Time: The Complete Interview—Live and Uncut!" *Reader's Digest*, 2001, http://docs.google.com/viewer?a=v&q=cache:gbGaTnrsidUJ:www.rd.com/images/content/101101/Paul_McCartney_interview.pdf+paul+mccartney+religion&hl=en&gl=us&pid=bl&srcid=AD-GEESiU_G_6epqsS0E6nXZy-ZE2c902kGwmpGwZPs24OE-JpPjWGT01rgkGsBv4wn8MtU4o9TpyT7ABM81vV5xVX-Mv8MZT-LaUZRi9SVz6RAd2ayduaQOVcozmzucDXLO-dG-fOTZQv1F&sig=AHIEtbTPgTsdBrusD1auAAqgxT3b0EuVsA.

9. Ibid.

10. "The God that I know and the God that I love will love me and love my children no matter what," August 24, 2010, dallasvoice.com, http://www.dallasvoice.com/the-god-god-love-love-love-children-matter-1040784.html.

11. Sarah Lyall, "George Harrison Stabbed in Chest by an Intruder," *New York Times*, December 31, 1999, http://www.nytimes.com/1999/12/31/world/george-harrison-stabbed-in-chest-by-an-intruder.html.

12. Ibid.

13. "Paul McCartney Discusses 'Blackbird Singing'" (transcript) CNN *Larry King Live*, aired June 12, 2001,
http://transcripts.cnn.com/TRANSCRIPTS/0106/12/lkl.00.html.

14. http://www.brainyquote.com/quotes/authors/l/linda_mccartney.html.

15. *White Anglo-Saxon Protestant*, or *WASP*, is an informal term, often

disparaging, for a closed group of high-status Americans, usually of British descent with a Protestant background.

16. *Linda McCartney: The Biography*, chap. 3, *Wingspan*, http://www. wingspan.ru/bookseng/linda/03.html.

17. Ibid.

18. Ibid.

19. "Paul McCartney Discusses 'Blackbird Singing.'"

20. Caris Davis, "Paul McCartney Opens Up about Final Moments with George Harrison," *People*, July 1, 2008, http://www.people.com/ people/article/0,,20209648,00.html.

21. Ibid.

22. http://beatlesquotes.com/paul-mccartney-quotes.htm.

23. Christian John Wikane, "Reflections of a Renaissance Man: An Interview with Paul McCartney," June 25, 2007, http://www. popmatters.com/pm/feature/reflections-of-a-renaissance-man-an-interview-with-paul-mccartney/.

24. Ibid.

25. Lennon-McCartney, "Eight Days a Week," 1964.

26. *Wikipedia*, s.v., "God Only Knows," http://en.wikipedia.org/wiki/ God_Only_Knows/.

27. Ibid.

28. http://www.brainyquote.com/quotes/authors/p/paul_mccartney_2. html.

CHAPTER 13

1. Steve Turner, "John Lennon: A New Jesus?" http://www.beliefnet. com/Entertainment/Music/2006/08/John-Lennon-A-New-Jesus. aspx?p=1.

2. Much of the historical content of this chapter is taken from *Wikipedia*, s.v., "George Harrison," http://en.wikipedia.org/wiki/George_Harrison.

3. In 2001, on CNN's *Larry King Live*, Paul spoke of George's talent:

MCCARTNEY: The two of us were the main writers. George wrote "Something in the Way She Moves" and . . .

KING: Not bad.

MCCARTNEY: . . . "Here goes"—"Here Comes the Sun." "Something in the Way She Moves" is a Harrison song. Frank Sinatra used to call it his favorite Lennon-McCartney.

KING: He said it right here on this show.

MCCARTNEY: Did he?

KING: I said not Lennon-McCartney. One of his favorite all-time songs anywhere, "Something in the Way She Moves."
("Paul McCartney Discusses 'Blackbird Singing'")

4. "Paul McCartney Says George Harrison Was Like His 'Baby Brother,'" June 1, 2008, http://www.exposay.com/paul-mccartney-says-george-harrison-was-like-his-baby-brother/v/21288/.

5. "John Lennon *Playboy* Interview Pt 1," http://beatlesnumber9.com/lennonplayboy.html.

6. Marjorie Miller, "Ex-Beatle Harrison Hurt by Intruder at His Home," *Los Angeles Times*, December 31, 1999, http://articles.latimes.com/1999/dec/31/news/mn-49333.

7. Abram served only nineteen months for this brutal attack. ("Freed Beatle's Attacker Sorry," BBC News, July 5, 2002, http://news.bbc.co.uk/2/hi/uk_news/england/2096082.stm.)

CHAPTER 14

1. From *I Me Mine,* Harrison's autobiography.

2. http://www.hinduismtoday.com/modules/smartsection/item.php?itemid=1472. No longer accessible.

3. "The Life of George Harrison," http://beatlesnumber9.com/george.html.

4. "The Life of George Harrison," http://beatlesnumber9.com/george.html.

5. The 2004 version of the film drops this scene.

6. Quoted under the "Fair Use" law—for educational purposes: *Fair Use, and Circular 21, Reproductions of Copyrighted Works by Educators and Librarians.*

7. George Harrison, at a press conference in Los Angeles, 1974.

8. "Awaiting on You All," from the album *All Things Must Pass.* Quoted under *Fair Use, and Circular 21, Reproductions of Copyrighted Works by Educators and Librarians.*

9. "The Life of George Harrison" (from an interview in 1982).

10. To *genuflect* means to "bend the knee."

11. H. Thurston, *The Catholic Encyclopedia,* s.v., "Hail Mary" (New York: Robert Appleton Company, 1910), retrieved March 20, 2012, from New Advent: http://www.newadvent.org/cathen/07110b.htm.

12. *On the Web* (blog), http://www.otweb.com/phramework/pw/module/blog/index.php?id=488&t=Difference_between_grace_and_mercy.

13. Hari Quotes, compiled by Aya and Lee, http://www.macca-l.org/hariontour/hariquotes.htm.

14. There were approximately 200,000 unsolved murders in the United States during the 1990s.

15. Bhagavatam, XI, ch. XXII, quoted at http://www.hinduism.co.za/goodand1.htm.

16. "Sin" (from the teachings of Sri Ramana Maharshi), under the heading "The Bible and Sin": "Question: May We Read the Bible?" http://www.hinduism.co.za/sin.htm.

17. Swami Abhedananda, Ramakrishna Vedanta Math, "Good and Evil," http://www.hinduism.co.za/goodand1.htm.

18. Quoted on Subhamoy Das's "Harrison & Hinduism: Harrison's Idea of God & Reincarnation," http://hinduism.about.com/od/artculture/a/harrison_2.htm.

19. *The Beatles!* Special Commemorative Issue, p. 41.

CHAPTER 15

1. Turner, "John Lennon: A New Jesus?"

2. Much of the historical content in this chapter was gleaned from *Wikipedia*, s.v., "Ringo Starr," http://en.wikipedia.org/wiki/Ringo_Starr.

3. Bill Harry, *The Ringo Starr Encyclopedia* (London: Virgin Books, 2004), 44.

4. Sean Manning, *Rock and Roll Cagematch: Music's Greatest Rivalries, Decided* (Crown Publishing Group, 2008).

5. *Wikipedia*, "Ringo Starr."

6. Ibid.

7. "Ringo Starr Attended an Evangelical Church in Liverpool," *Christian Telegraph*, http://www.christiantelegraph.com/issue8593.html.

8. The Internet Beatles Album, "Reference Library: John and Ringo Interview," http://www.beatlesagain.com/breflib/jandr.html.

9. The Beatles Website, "John and Ringo Interview," August 23, 1964, http://www.thebeatleswebsite.com/documents/randj1964.html.

10. Ben Todd, "Why I've Turned to God at 70, by Reformed Ringo Starr . . . That's 44 Years after Lennon Said the Beatles Were Bigger Than Jesus," *Mail Online* (UK), February 3, 2010, http://www.dailymail.co.uk/tvshowbiz/article-1248085/Why-Ive-turned-God-70-reformed-Ringo-Starr.html.

11. "Ringo Starr Attended an Evangelical Church in Liverpool," *Christian Telegraph*, http://www.christiantelegraph.com/print.php?id=8593.

12. Andrew Hough, "Ringo Starr Admits: 'I Have Found God,'" *Independent Woman*, February 3, 2010, http://www.independent.ie/lifestyle/independent-woman/celebrity-news-gossip/ringo-starr-

admits-i-have-found-god-2045377.html.

13. For more on *mens rea*, see http://legal-dictionary.thefreedictionary.
com/mens+rea.

14. http://youtu.be/RLozc5DY-UQ.

15. John Lennon, interviewed by David Sheff, Playboy, April 1981 edition, p 192

LENNON-MCCARTNEY TIMELINE

1. http://www.angelfire.com/stars/LennonMcCartney/page2.html.

Last Will and Testament of John Winston Ono Lennon
1. http://www.john-lennon.com/johnlennon.htm.

APPENDIX

1. Jennifer Harper, "Study: Americans Pray Just to Get Through the Day," *Washington Times*, December 5, 2008, http://www.washingtontimes.com/news/2008/dec/05/study-americans-pray-just-to-get-through-the-day/.

Index

In *Hitler, God, and the Bible*, international evangelist and best-selling author Ray Comfort exposes Adolf Hitler's theology and abuse of religion as a means to seize political power and ultimately instigate World War II and genocide.

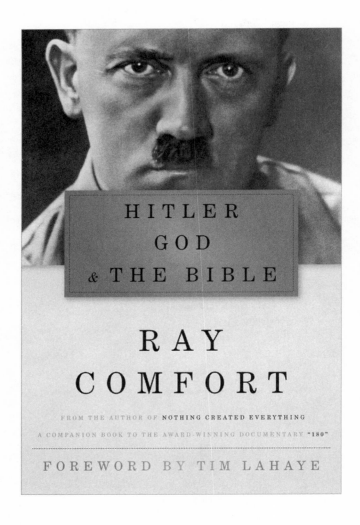

HITLER
GOD
& THE BIBLE

RAY
COMFORT

FROM THE AUTHOR OF **NOTHING CREATED EVERYTHING**

A COMPANION BOOK TO THE AWARD-WINNING DOCUMENTARY "180"

FOREWORD BY TIM LAHAYE

WND BOOKS

WND Books • a WND Company • Washington, DC • www.wndbooks.com